LightHeart Books ━━

Once Around the Wheel

Want To Go Again?

*Life, Death, Healing,
Transformation,
and Life Again*

LYNNE RICH

LightHeart Books

Once Around the Wheel
Want To Go Again?
Life, Death, Healing, Transformation, and Life Again
by **Lynne Rich**

Copyright © 1996 Lynne Rich

ISBN: 1-888207-00-0
LC: 95-81030

Publisher:

LightHeart Books
P. O. Box 2430-1009
Pensacola, FL 32513-2430

Interior and Cover Design: Betsy A. Lampe

Retail Price: $12.99

Manufactured in the United States of America

Dedication _____

To Judy Collins,
whose exquisite voice is
the Voice of Everywoman
and whose songs
have been the music of my life.

Blessed Be.

Acknowledgments

My heartfelt thanks to my goddess-self and my dog-self.

My dog-self, in the very real form of Winks, reminded me to take play breaks and kept me warm through a very cold winter. My goddess-self whispered, sometimes almost inaudibly, the words of encouragement I so desperately needed to keep taking the next step.

Together, they carried me through a very dark tunnel into the light.

Contents ━━━━━━━━━━━

Introduction _____

I was born on June twenty-second, the calendar date that corresponds to the first key in the major arcana of the Tarot, the cards depicting fate and divine legacy.

The first key is the Fool and is represented by a zero. The Fool is the journeyer and mediator between all the other twenty-one keys. Taken as a whole, the keys of the major arcana represent all the archetypes and experiences of life. The Fool's purpose is to experience and become each of the other keys. The journey of the Fool includes learning to create reality patterns by becoming the Magician, Key One, to learning the secrets of the past and future by becoming the High Priestess, Key Two, and on through the complete path where the Fool must return to the Source. Perfect zero, the Source, represents all possibility. It is emptiness that, within the void, holds all creativity.

The purpose of the Fool's journey is to seek understanding of all the components of the human psyche as well as that which is beyond the human psyche, all the mysteries of life. The Fool journeys for the sake of the journey, for the sake of the experience, for the sake of understanding. The Fool is trusting and journeys without judgement. The Fool risks because the Fool has faith in the positive forces that offer protection. The Fool is always innocent and always loves. The Fool is a Child of the Universe.

Some who are less innocent and trusting, say the Fool is naive. The Fool's belief in the rightness and goodness of others is sometimes perceived as idiocy or childishness. The Fool is sometimes perceived as an easy target. But the Fool is not naive. The Fool is acutely aware. Yet, to the Fool, all things are equal. That is why the Fool never misses anything.

At full circle, the Fool must begin anew, this time acting as translator and mediator to all the other keys. Yet, from the beginning of the next journey, and through each successive experience on the path, the Fool is always acutely aware that the Fool is ever the Fool.

Though I wrote this book with a wide spectrum of people in mind, I imagine it will be most appealing to those of you who stand at a crossroads in your life. It is a bootstrappers book, a "How To Pick Yourself Up, Dust Yourself Off, and Start All Over Again" book with a twist. The idea is not to do it all over again but to make it up the way you want it the second time around. The book is about rediscovering who you are and understanding the seamless connection you have to others and to All. This is a book about power — your personal power. In some ways it is a metaphysical book in that it deals with ideas that take us beyond physical facts. It is also a practical book that contains simple steps and concepts.

We are standing in the doorway to a new age. The transition from the Age of Pisces to the Age of Aquarius holds much promise for each of us and for our planet. It is an in-between time of much letting go and much looking ahead. For many this is a time of major life shifts and changes accompanied by real loss, grief, and sorrow. Many not undergoing actual life transitions, are, nonetheless, reexperiencing feelings from old or unresolved losses buried in the subconscious. There is everywhere a sense of sorrow and grief, a pause between the letting go of an old phase and the push forward into a new phase. This is a book about that transition and the importance of this time as a healing phase.

From my personal experience and my work with colleagues, clients, and associates, I am convinced that the greatest area in need of healing is the feminine energy in all of us. If we could heal only one aspect of our human energy, the feminine, emotional energy holds the most promise for individual and global transformation.

Part I of this book, Endings/Beginnings, gives you an idea of where I am coming from and some background on the foundation concepts of this book. Part II, Healing, outlines a wide range of effective healing approaches. Part III, Transformation, outlines steps to personal transformation. I have included, within Parts II and III, my experience with and observations about the women's movement, popular music, and the overall dysfunctional state of our cultural institutions.

I did not write this book with only women in mind; though the book is written by a woman and it certainly speaks from a woman's experience. I think my life path has enabled me to strike a fairly good balance between my feminine and masculine energies and my words speak to both my sisters and brothers.

I have been and done a lot in my forty-eight years. Some of my experiences come from my having been a daughter, a sister, a lover, a friend, a mate, a counselor, a corporate executive for twenty years, a Girl Scout camp director, a political activist, a writer, a musician, a singer, an organic gardener, a traveler, an astrologer for almost thirty years, a trainer, and an ever-curious student. My life has included some tremendous successes and some stunning failures. I like the successes best; but the failures taught me the most.

It is my pleasure to share with you my discoveries. I speak from my experience, from what is true for me. In understanding my life purpose as a teacher, I share some of my experiences with you. We are each on a different path. Each of us has a unique life pattern. My way is not your way; yours is not mine. I have a great respect for that. We do, however, share some common experiences by virtue of our being human together. I offer this book as a gift to you. Take what is useful and helpful. Take what supports your own healing and transformation.

I have been once around the wheel. I am preparing to go again.

Early in my writing of this book, Moonwinks, a female miniature schnauzer puppy came into my life. She's here as my guide. I hope Winks and I see you in our travels.

Love,
The Fool

Part 1

Endings/Beginnings

Introduction —————————————

I will spare the details of how it all started, for now. It will all come out, or "unfold," as we say, over the next pages. I will cut to the chase and you will get it as we go along.

I had a little visit with a well-known psychic. I have been having a lot of my own "psychic flashes" along with my hot flashes. According to how I saw it, my life had just about ended. I am on the verge of being forty-eight years old and everything, but everything, in my life is done, gone, finished or completed. Over the course of the last four years, I have experienced many losses and endings. Enough that, to my way of experiencing it, it was all gone.

As a professional astrologer, I knew that, for me, Pluto had wiped the slate clean. I had died. I simply had not left my physical body yet. At the same time, I also knew it was possible to have a second "incarnation" with the same physical body. Some people get three and four incarnations crammed into one physical lifespan.

While I have been letting go of all the attachment

to my old incarnation, I have also been preparing for the possibility of another incarnation in case I do not leave my physical body this year. Mind you, it is not that I want to leave my physical body on this Pluto transit. I just wanted to be prepared, in case.

So, for a couple of months, I declared myself "in transition". I was letting go, feeling my pain, getting my balance and healing. I was taking whatever time it was supposed to take to experience my pain, hurt, anger, grief and sorrow. I reached out for and accepted as many different kinds of healing as possible. I think, for the first time ever, I let myself experience being needy.

All the while, the intensity of my psychic flashes increased. Amazingly, the more I let go and detached, the more the psychic channels opened.

I wanted to trust what was happening but I had such trust "issues". Did not a lot of my past life experiences revolve around trusting too much, wanting to trust, and, in the end, not trusting myself? Yet I was beginning to actually materialize real things. Some of the things, people, and opportunities looked like real miracles to me. I realized how much and how often I used my abilities to manifest things for others in my past incarnation. It seemed I could always use my magical abilities to get things for other people. Now, and, at last, it felt like I was starting to be my own metaphysical magician.

Time for a second opinion . . .

I was greeted at the door by a black, female miniature schnauzer. Her name was Zoe and she was a year old. I said that that was exactly the kind of dog I had begun looking for. Pamela White gave me the name of the breeder and said I should call right away. She was very matter of fact and, at the same time, quite definite.

As I settled on her couch, she said, "You've been here before but I don't know you. My people know you".

I had been to her three years before. I didn't like what she told me then. Much of it was more what she didn't say. But she was very accurate and I had a great deal of respect for her ability and integrity as a psychic. I also knew she intuitively perceived information through "her people" whom I understood to be a combination of her spirit support team and those from spirit the client brought along.

From her easychair across the room, Pamela White started to speak, then covered her eyes briefly, and finally said, "You are somehow tied up. I'm getting more of a symbol here. I'm seeing a blindfold. Somehow you have blinders on."

Knowing she works through voice contact, I spoke clearly, "Not anymore"

"But you are tied up in some situation"

I sensed this might be about my preoccupation with letting go. "I am in a transition from one life to another. Almost everything in my past life of almost forty-eight years is gone. I've lost through death or separation almost everyone in my life. It is a personal death experience for me and I am looking at recreating a new life."

"It is not a death but a whole new chapter," she said. "And everyone isn't gone. Those in spirit are very much with you."

Before my appointment with Pamela White, I attended a short spiritual message service in one of the churches on the grounds of this spiritual community. There was a message for me. The speaker told me that I should understand that there really was no death, only the movement from the physical to the spiritual plane. She said she could clearly see an angel at my shoulder who was a very strong angel for me. She asked did I know who it was?

"Yes, I do." I smiled at the speaker and for myself. What a comfort to know my mother was showing up with such presence. Not that I was surprised. She was always such a presence on the earth plane.

Now, from her easychair, Pamela White said, "They want you to know its time for you to speak. Everything has been opened up and cleared for you to act. You have been through a lot of loss and pain . . ."

I started to react. She put up her hand and said, "I don't feel any excuses for you. You have suffered more than most it is true. But," she smiled, "you are stronger than most."

I laughed out loud. I could not help it. I had had a love/hate relationship with the notion that I was "stronger than most" all my life. I immediately knew that one of "the people" she gave voice to was my mother. It made me laugh more. It was laughter that comes from knowing. It was also, in a peculiar way, relief.

"You are not alone. You have some very powerful people in spirit. I'm getting a lot for you today from, is it your mother?"

"You bet," I said, "and she's pretty solidly here." I outlined my mother's presence around my shoulders.

Pamela White started to explain about death and the spirit plane but stopped. She looked at me and said,

"But you know all this. In fact, you know all about metaphysics. What do you do?"

I answered, "I'm a professional astrologer. Actually, I set my practice aside for six years and I'm rebuilding, recreating".

"There's no need to rebuild or recreate," she said. "It is all there for you. You haven't lost anything so there's no need to rebuild. Just do it." This was the first of many times she used that phrase and it reminded me of the commercial slogan for running shoes. Then she said again, "There are no excuses."

I told the psychic I had become aware of how, in the past, I made a great distinction in my astrology practice between being intuitive and being psychic. I always said I was not a psychic but used a lot of intuition in my practice of astrology. With the increasing amount and intensity of psychic experiences in recent months, I was beginning to rethink this.

Once again, she raised her hand like a stop sign. "There is no difference for you. Intuitive. Psychic. Call it what you will. You are a psychic. You use astrology as your channel. It is that simple. Don't complicate it. JUST DO IT."

I wanted to explore with her how I might get better in touch with my inner guidance and psychic knowing.

"I have a problem with Inner Guidance and going within," she said. "For you, there is no need to go within anymore. If you mean trust what is within, well, you got it," she laughed, " and you know it. So JUST DO IT. But you know it is from outside you now. It is everywhere you are and, for you, especially in nature." She said that in such a way that I clearly understood the nature trip wasn't especially her route.

"My people are telling me, I'm getting this strongly, that you already know everything you need to know to do what you have to do now. This new chapter in your life, this second half, is what everything in the first half of your life has prepared you for. You need to do it now. I see a couple of books and a lot of teaching. You have to take what you've got, and you have so much, believe me. I don't tell this to everyone. I am even running past my time with you and I do it gladly. Your life is about giving it out. Teaching, sharing your experience, giving what you know to others. Don't question your life up to now. You gave until there was nothing left. But you had to do that. For one thing, the life experiences you have now give so much depth and compassion to your work."

"Being the perfectionist that you are, you've done it so well. You did your twenty four year relationship really well, except that maybe you didn't end it soon enough." I laughed at this and she said, "But you did everything that you had to do and you did it well. As far as all the losses of the past four years, you needed all of it. You needed to be set absolutely free to do what you need to do. Now get on with it. JUST DO IT."

"As far as your ex-partner goes, you got on very different paths. You grew in very different directions. Or, well, you kept growing. You needed to break out, break free, and you let your loyalty get in the way. But what about your loyalty to yourself and the work you know you must do?"

"Your mother, here in spirit, is telling me she will help you in the work. You have others helping you also, a grandmother." Pamela White finished speaking and sat back in her chair. I smiled and felt relieved. I was getting a real solid second opinion. I do know what I know.

We discussed some decisions I needed to make, some health issues I needed to handle, and directions I needed to follow. She emphatically told me I do not need to be a student anymore. "I know you enjoy learning. For you life is one long learning adventure. And, don't stop that. For you that's fun," she laughed, "your kind of fun. You are always the curious child and that's great. But you don't need to learn anymore to do what you have to do. Teach it, share it, write about it. You already have so much. Get on with it," and now she caught herself and laughed as she said, "Just do it."

"It is time for you to speak," rang in my ears. The psychic also asked if there was a book I was writing. I told her that, in fact, I was gathering information for a resource book on transition and change. She told me to continue with that project, but that there was another book.

When I said I was looking for clues to further developing my psychic abilities, she answered my question with a question? "How do you think you do it?" I gave her the answer I thought was the way, the only way, the way I had read about, practiced all my life, studied, meditated over and, with my whole heart, believed in, "Go within".

Her response was direct, immediate and straight-forward. "No. Go Without. You don't need to go within anymore. For you, it is time to go outside." It hit me right between the eyes. I could actually feel it connect with that spot between the eyes we call the Third Eye, the place of seeing and knowing.

I knew that I knew what she had told me. "Go out-side" was a voice I had heard for several months. The force had been so strong, that I had been following it on a very literal level. At every opportunity I had been "going outside". I had become so aware of a deep physical need for sunshine, warmth, and movement that, at times, I could do nothing else until I satisfied that need. I had begun to joke about my body being a solar cell that needed recharging. It felt good to be aware of my physical needs. I was delighted, even blissful, in experiencing how simple it was to take care of my needs and take care of myself.

"It is time for you to speak." "Go outside. Go With-out." "Another book." I let it all roll around in my head for a while.

As I drove through the countryside that day, I had a wonderful sense of knowing. I felt crystal clear and peaceful. I understood all the opposites, dualities, and contradictions in my life and in the universe.

Earlier in my life I had had a couple of experiences of "enlightenment" when it all made sense and I had a glimpse at my own completeness and the whole-ness of the universe. But they were only glimpses. With time and life's experiences, I went unconscious to my enlightened understanding.

This time I knew it was different. I would no longer go unconscious to what I knew and understood. This time I had moved my entire being into the light of knowing.

It was a bright, warm, and powerful place to be and I knew that, from now on, I would choose to live in the light.

Opposites, Dualities, and Contradictions

This is my story. This is my truth.

Some of my labels are psychic, guide, sharer. I am forty-eight years old and I know that every moment in my life has led to this moment. Until now, I have not been much of a "big picture" person, I experienced all the endings, losses, and pain of the past four years as death. All around me was death and dying and I experienced my own death along with it.

I had come to believe that I had lived a complete lifetime and died without leaving my physical body. In this way I was being given the opportunity to choose a second lifetime and recreate myself.

My psychic friend told me that it was not death that I had experienced but the clearing out of all attachments so I could get on with what I was meant to do. She said it was not the end of one life but the beginning of a new chapter with the optimal chance for a fresh start.

At first, I resisted this new perspective. I realized I had invested a lot of energy over past months in my "dying without leaving my physical body" experience.

And, surely, the physical, mental, emotional, and spiritual pain I felt was as real as death could be.

Yet I was also coming to understand that, in clinging to the notion of my "dying without leaving my physical body" I also had to accept the death of my past life of forty-eight years. To really die, I needed to completely let go of everything, including my past.

I had been consciously letting go for a couple of months. I was also becoming increasingly aware of my resistance to completely let go of my past. I knew that complete detachment from my past was the ultimate step in freeing myself for recreation. At the same time, I was acutely aware of how many of my good and positive experiences would have to be sacrificed to this process.

It did not take long for me to see that, once again, I understood another contradiction. As I looked at my resistance to seeing not my death but a new chapter, I realized that it was both.

The death I had experienced was very real. But I could not and would not allow my complete past to die. I wanted all the good from my past, as well as all the lessons. In this way, and, for the first time, I could clearly see the "big picture." Experiencing myself beginning a new chapter allowed me to have a sense of continuity. I could still grieve my losses yet I could cherish and honor all the good. I could also keep my "dying without leaving my physical body" experience. It was useful to me when I did my work with recreating myself.

There are many ways of knowing one's own truth. For me, as an astrologer, most of my knowing and understanding comes clear within astrology's language of symbols. I see in terms of my understanding of the patterns and pictures. When I sit down with a client and put the birthchart before me, I know that person. The chart is my crystal ball. In that time, while I am with the client, my psychic channel opens wide.

I have learned to respect the language of astrology. In some ways, it is a funny language. Although, what you see is what is there, things are not always what they appear to be. The language, at times, is like The Trickster. It is always exactly what you see and, at the same time, it has a completely separate side.

In my new awareness, I was both fascinated and frightened by the fact that I had always had an innate understanding of contradictions and dualities. Why did I go unconscious? Why did I cut myself off from myself? Why was I now uncovering what I already knew, always had known. I had forgotten things I understood perfectly well in childhood.

I believe, and have always shared with my clients, that we choose our lives, our birthcharts, our unique patterns and destinies. Most of the time this is met with "You gotta be kidding, I would never choose this for myself". Yet, on some level, I know most people can accept this.

There is, however, an interesting thing that happens in the process of a spirit energy choosing a specific birth moment and birth situation. Once the spirit energy enters a physical body, it forgets all the good reasons why it chose that life. The very act of a spiritual entity merging with a physical body, human birth, sets up a very interesting dynamic. A big part of being human is forgetting, or going unconscious, to everything we know as pure spirit. Being human, and acting human is the process of uncovering and remembering what we already know.

We have to respect that we knew what we were doing in spirit when we chose this particular lifetime. We have to take responsibility for living our lives. We have to accept that the spiritual part of us knows and understands everything. We have to commit to moving into, then staying in the light.

It is difficult for many to accept the idea of choosing and creating their lives and circumstances. The temptation to judge the past becomes very great. All the faults, failures, losses, and pain can come flooding to the surface. The burden can seem heavy indeed. Discovering that you chose, in fact, created, your own circumstances can come as a nasty surprise. Accepting only this side of the duality creates guilt and regret. Believing only that you chose your life pattern and created your own circumstances is dangerous and destructive.

While it is true that you must be responsible for the life you chose, you must also remember that, as soon as you were born, you started to forget. Your spiritual side knows the "gameplan" and your spirit is a perfectionist. Moment-to-moment your life unfolds perfectly. In understanding this there is, then, no self-blame and no self-judgement. This is the gentle way to live. This is the responsible way to live. This is the way to treat yourself with kindness, respect and understanding.

Most things in this world are not black or white, one or the other. Most things are both. In the seed of one thing is its opposite. A lot of what we do in our lives and how we experience our lives depends on our ability to see the value in opposites, dualities, and contradictions. In trying to understand our lives and circumstances, we constantly struggle for resolutions. In order to move on, we feel we need to label our lessons and grade our experiences.

In my own struggle to come to terms with the end of a twenty-four-year relationship, I found myself smack in the middle of this either/or dilemma. This relationship had been the framework of my entire adult life. I was twenty-four and full of dreams and ideas about the future. I had met my soulmate. We shared the same vision. I wanted to spend the rest of my life with this woman. I wanted to fulfill every dream and gracefully grow old together.

I spent the long and painful months of the breakup struggling with my own denial. The acceptance phase was fraught with traps for me. In order to accept that it was really over, I became consumed by my need to put the relationship, that represented my whole life, in some kind of perspective. I needed to resolve it. I needed to put it in a box, label it, and put it away on a shelf. I fought myself at every turn. For a short while, I was convinced that I would never be able to heal unless I understood.

My enlightenment about understanding it all is that you cannot understand it all. I knew I had to hold my need to figure it out along with my understanding that you can't figure it out. If I chose either one of these two opposites, I would do myself harm. I realized I can keep my need to figure it out as long as I understand that I can't figure it all out. This, may seem like circular logic; but, the more you deny something you need, in my case the need to figure it out, the stronger the need becomes. By acknowledging my need to understand, and acknowledging that it, ultimately, cannot be understood, I put myself in a gentle space. Accepting the opposites, dualities, and contradictions moves us into a place of self-acceptance.

In time and in many ways, I came to know the truth about myself, my life path, and my life purpose. I am here as a teacher. Everything in my life, Part I, has led me to this very moment. My original gift, the talent in my birth chart, is the innate understanding of the human psyche. I had used the gift well; but the gift of understanding involves the mind only. To teach in the way I was meant to teach involves knowing with the heart. Knowing with the heart can only come from experiencing the wholistic involvement of body, mind, feelings, and spirit.

In order to experience the full range of the human psyche, the path of my last four or so years was defined by the influence of the planet Pluto, the symbolic energy of death, loss, and destruction. The dying, destructiveness, and losses in my outside world perfectly reflected my inner world. In my final surrender to Pluto, I gave up when I could go no more and experienced my own dying. In the experience of dying came my knowing Pluto's potential for recreation.

I had always understood the nature of opposites, dualities, and contradictions. Through my experience I now knew the nature of these things. Within each experience is completely contained its opposite. Out of total darkness comes light. Out of emptiness comes fullness. Out of total loss of control comes freedom.

Confusion

What's all this fuss about confusion? We act as if confusion is some kind of imbalance that should only be suffered by other, less intelligent persons. In our society, confusion is considered to be a sign of weakness. No one should be confused or, at least, should ever admit that they are confused. People who are confused about something are considered slow or dim. We live in an instant world where everyone is required to "get it" immediately. There is enormous outside pressure to quickly absorb the facts and, then, make instant decisions. The high-tech computer age has only increased the pressure. Information is accessible and instant. Now there is really no excuse for delay.

In my own transition period, the time where I got to focus on healing my past and recreating my future, one of the things I realized was how much I had always enjoyed analyzing and figuring things out. Through most of my life I have been on a self-actualization quest. I participated in many self-development programs and practices. I found personal value in each of them. I have gotten answers and "ah-ha's" many times over.

It is a great game to play "figure it all out". My mother and I often played the game together. We used to call it "solving all the problems of the world". My partner and I played it and we were quite good at it.

Through my awareness of my need to understand opposites, dualities, and contradictions, I realized that, this need was, in the past, a fun game for me. Yet, in a lot of ways, it had served its purpose. I remembered the times when the game took too much of my energy, when I put too much into it, when it felt like a struggle. I came to the conclusion that, for me, I could still enjoy the "figure it all out" game. When the game got too rough on me, when it felt like hard work, I would simply stop, let it go, and take a break. Outside pressures are only that. Inner peace and moving with your natural flow are the only things that really matter.

A friend, who is a very compassionate healer, recently said, "I don't understand why my clients think they aren't supposed to be confused. They fight themselves. They put so much darned energy into it. Then they come to me to learn to relax. It all seems backwards. I love confusion. It gives me a chance to be with a thing for awhile, sort of play with it, then send it Out There. When I do this before I go to sleep, usually, the next morning, I awake with an answer, or, at least a clue. It works all the time."

Here's the big news. Confusion is perfectly natural and necessary. Confusion appears when you try to push the timing of a decision that is not ready to be made. Confusion comes from trying to control outcomes. When you exert too much effort and try too hard, confusion arises. The resulting frustration is your attempt at trying to swim against the tide, the timing tide.

You can quite easily eliminate the frustration that accompanies confusion by letting go and detaching from the matter at hand. Release it. Recognize that the flow, the tide, and the timing will produce natural, easy results. The harder, more difficult the problem, the more your release should be light and easy.

In this world of "make a decision yesterday," dare to be different. Dare to be true to yourself. Take your time. Take all the time you need. Accept the naturalness of confusion. It is a timer that sets the ebb and flow of your life. You have a right to all the confusion you need.

Breakdown, Breakout, Breakthrough

In my work with clients over the years, and in my own experience, I have noticed that life transitions, especially major life transitions, are marked by distinct phases. Each person's experience of these phases is different. The timing varies. And some people get stuck in a phase, usually the first phase.

Major life transitions, those involving heavy losses of people and personal identity, always have a *breakdown period*. In the case of a sudden loss due to death, the breakdown period may be short but is usually acute. Other types of breakdowns, often relationship breakdowns, occur over the course of months or years. One's experience of the breakdown may be as if it is happening out of the blue. The swiftness of events that occur during this kind of breakdown often cause shock and panic. Another's experience of a breakdown may be feeling things sliding out of control, almost as if it is happening in slow motion. The reaction to this kind of breakdown is often helplessness and depression. Career losses are often experienced this way.

Not all major life transitions require a *breakout*

phase, but most do. This is the phase that requires us to take some action. Often it requires courageous action. Sometimes it is, quite literally, the only way to save yourself, to survive. The breakout phase takes a lot of energy and personal strength. It comes right on top of an often exhausting breakdown period, so the situation is compounded.

The breakout phase was the most difficult time period of my life. Over the course of four years everything in my life had broken down. I had literally come to the end of my rope. I had crashed into all my walls. I knew I was going down for the third time and there was no one to save me but myself. I knew it would take enormous strength to put the brakes on and stop my own pain. No one wanted to hear me.

The breakdown had sapped all my energy and I did not think I had the strength to break out. Everything in my life had become interconnected. Breaking out meant stopping love, work, and caregiving. It meant losing my partner, my social circle, my extended family, my pets, and my income. It meant stopping the work and the political activism that had become my life for the past several years. I had been half of a highly visible and outwardly successful couple. We were often referred to as the "dynamic duo" and served as role models for long-term relationships. Breaking out meant losing my identity.

It took four months to get our lives untangled and separated. It blurs together now as four months of pure pain. It was four months of denial and resistance from everywhere I turned. Long before my partner moved herself and her offices out of the house, I felt abandoned. Everyone said that what I had to do was the hardest thing they could think of and then they backed away and disappeared. I lost thirty-five pounds and my new identity was a walking wall of pain.

Facing the emptiness in my life felt like a new bottom. When everything broke down four months earlier, I tried to stop the pain by breaking out. I had begun to regain a sense of myself. In the midst of the most stormy period of my life, I started to realize there was still a center, a core of strength in me that had the will to keep going; but I had lost my spiritual connection.

My life was a four month struggle for survival. Then, four months later, the emptiness felt like I did not survive at all. For weeks it felt like death. The physical, mental, emotional, and spiritual pain was death.

Early in the breakout phase I had already begun to reach out for help in anticipation of my need for major healing. In my mind, I believed recovery was possible, but I feared I did not have the energy or strength to go the full route which I understood to take a long time, in my case, maybe years. The time and effort it would take just to recover and declare myself a survivor did not seem worth it. Yet I knew I had little choice other than to stay on the path of healing.

Somewhere in the middle of resigning myself to continue my healing and sorting out and clearing out the wreckage that remained in my life, I began to experience a *breakthrough*.

The breakthrough was more like a series of small voices at first, then there were louder psychic flashes. I immediately understood that, to the extent that your life was in disarray, disruption, and turmoil, the greater the possibility for transformation. To the extent that your old beliefs and cherished ideals have been smashed, the greater the possibility for seeing truth. When the slate has been wiped clean, there is enormous potential for new growth.

As soon as I began to accept what I was sensing, I began to experience myself as a clear channel. The voice of guidance comes through in many ways. I understood that transformation is about making a choice. I had always known and understood about transformation and enlightenment. Why did I forget? I finally remembered that my spirit had good reasons for it all when it chose this life pattern. Its just that when spirit links up with the physical body, the resulting "humanness" makes us tend to forget. I chose transformation and acceptance of the beginning of my own healing process.

Universal Energy: The Web_____

Everything in the Universe is interconnected. Everything is of the one Universal Energy. We personalize the one Universal Energy and refer to it by many names. God, the Goddess, Mother-Father God, the Higher Power and Allah are but a few of these names. Each is a form of our personal acknowledgment of a Divine Universal Energy. From the tiniest atomic particle to the mighty solar system, *everything is an expression of the one Universal Energy that exists as a web of interconnection.*

Within the Universal Energy web, each thing is whole and complete in itself and in its representation of Universal Energy. Each thing, in itself, is complete. Each of us, as ourselves, are complete. Each of us is part of and interconnected to the whole.

Universal Energy is all of physical energy, the material, and nonphysical energy, the spiritual. In total, it is neither good nor bad, but neutral; it contains all positivity and all negativity, all light and all darkness. And, while Universal Energy contains all of these opposites, the energy always exists as pure potential.

Universal Energy, the potential of all forces, has only

two qualities: motion and change. The only certainty in the Universe, then, is motion and change. Not death, not taxes; but motion and change.

Human beings have the ability to affect the Universal Energy potential. It is our two uniquely human characteristics of *conscious awareness* and *choice* that are our power. In fact, it is the purpose of being human to affect Universal Energy. As vital components of the Universal Energy web, it is our responsibility to act upon the potential of Universal Energy. Our purpose is to, individually and collectively, operate as generators and directors of the Universal Energy potential. We tap into and activate the energy through our powers of conscious awareness and choice.

It is our nature and purpose to act upon the potential of Universal Energy. It is our responsibility, to ourselves and everything else in the universe, to use our abilities of conscious awareness and choice for right and good purposes. Since the only certainty in the Universe is motion and change, we humans must attune and align ourselves with motion and change as we act upon the great potential energy. As we become sensitive and responsive to timing and our connectedness to a universal rhythm, we go with the flow. We then become co-creators of our world and everything in it.

To operate unconsciously is to be at the effect of movement and change. To make no choice is to choose the randomness of Universal motion and change. Those who operate unconsciously are often dangerous to themselves and others. Those who do not use the ability of conscious awareness and choice for right and good purposes act irresponsibly and are dangerous to themselves and others. We need only look back over the past fifty years to find numerous examples of the misuse of our human gifts.

What we are really talking about here is power. The human abilities of conscious awareness and choice are power, the personal power in each of us. This is the personal power to co-create our world. Misuse of the abilities is the misuse of power. All things, all beings, and all energy forms are interconnected in the web. One person's misuse of power has far reaching ramifications. The right and good use of Universal Energy is a serious thing. We cannot escape our responsibility to co-create our own lives and we cannot hide from awareness that all we do affects everything else.

While there may be other beings in the universe who share the responsibility, we cannot assume anything or we shirk our responsibility. I like to believe there are other beings operating in concert with humans; but I do not know for sure. What I do know is that we humans have responsibility to affect Universal Energy, it is our job; and I hope we are getting help.

Movement and change in the Universe operate by the law of balance, Universal Karma. In the big picture, the timeless Universe is always in perfect balance and harmony with all of its light energy and all of its dark energy. At the same time, we humans are saddled with the notions of time and space. We create according to our human perspective and we have the ability to create crisis and chaos for ourselves and our planet or balance and harmony. According to the human perception of time, we need to act to affect the planet now.

Mirror Reflections _____

While all things in the Universe are interrelated, each thing is also a perfect miniature of the whole. The Universe reflects, on a grand scale, a mirror image of life on Planet Earth. Life on Planet Earth reflects the status of the Universe. In astrology, the mirror reflection, is captured in the phrase, "As Above, So Below". The macrocosm reflects the microcosm and the microcosm reflects the macrocosm.

Your birthchart is a mirror reflection of the pattern of the sky at the time of your birth. The planets, signs of the Zodiac, and their location in the sections or houses of the wheel of life form an accurate image of your uniqueness and completeness in this incarnation. Your "hor-o-scope" is the scope or projection of the hour or moment you were born and came into physical form. Your horoscope, or birthchart, is a blueprint and, as such, is static. It is a picture of all the potential for you in this lifetime. The planets reflect the nature of Universal Energy in that their only certainty is movement and change. As the planets move throughout the heavens, each planet, in its own time and in its own orbit, influences your original pattern and unlocks your potential. The timing and influence reflects your unique pattern unfolding.

Metaphysically, mirror reflection can be seen in the principle of synchronicity — all things are synchronized and reflections of all other things. There is no chance. Nothing is serendipitous. All things, people, situations, and circumstances are purposeful. It is, of course, up to you to assert your human abilities of conscious awareness and choice, your personal power. It is up to you to claim the potential energy of all the things, people, situations, and circumstances in your life for your own right and good purposes.

Psychologically, we know that the outer person is a reflection of the inner person; the inner person a reflection of the outer person — as within, so without. We create from within. The creation of your life is an inside job. *As a co-creator of your own life, everything around you is a mirror reflection of the life you have created.* Whether you have been active or passive in the creation, you, nonetheless, own the creation. Your lifestyle, relationships, and environment are all the product of your creation. What does the mirror reflect back to you?

The nature of Universal Energy guarantees that movement and change are inevitable in your life. If you do not like something in your life, you can choose to just wait it out, for change will surely happen. You can subject yourself to the randomness of change and life happens to you. Unless you assert your powers of conscious awareness and choice, life happens and shit happens, and you operate at the affect of it all.

To be fully alive and responsible to yourself, others, and all things in the Universal web, exercise your power of conscious awareness and choice to recreate your world. Rebuild your life on right and good purposes and leave your positive imprint on the Universal web.

Part II

Healing

Introduction

Healing is a process of restoring yourself to wholeness, to your original innocence. The healing process involves reestablishing a balance between your original mind, body, spirit, and emotions. The healing process restores your unique, individual harmony. The process requires taking time for yourself and your own "hands-on" and self-directed energy. It requires that you take a leap of faith and trust that the original you can reappear.

Each of us is a precious and innocent child. We are each perfect, complete, and different from each other. I have had the benefit of looking at thousands of clients' birthcharts over the years; I know that no two people are exactly alike. We are truly like snowflakes, no two the same. What a wonderful way for Father Sky and Mother Earth, our Godparents, to express themselves. No two people are exactly alike, yet each of us is the same in that we are all perfect expressions of our Godparents. Healing is the return to your original wholeness. It is the freeing of your own perfect self-expression. It is an ongoing and lifelong process of establishing and reestablishing your own perfect balance.

Healing and transformation are two separate processes yet they are interrelated. While it is possible to achieve personal healing alone, it is not possible to achieve personal transformation without personal healing. Your commitment to personal transformation first requires a commitment to personal healing. The processes can then be simultaneous. Neither healing nor transformation is a one shot deal. If you commit to both the healing and the transformation process, your commitment is to an ongoing process, a process of becoming more and more of you.

The personal healing process focuses on balance. When the elements within you are in balance, you experience healing and well-being. The elements; fire, earth, air, and water correspond to your spirit, body, mind, and emotions.

Astrological symbols in your birthchart provide an important key to understanding your own unique pattern. The twelve signs of the zodiac are divided into the four elemental groupings of fire, earth, air, and water. Your birthchart, the pattern of the sky at the time of your birth, reflects the natural mix of elements in your individual pattern. Here again, we are all different. Some of us have a preponderance of fire energy; while others have more natural earth energy. Some of us chose (remember choosing?) patterns with an equal mix of the elements; while others chose patterns with little or no natural energy in certain elements.

Those of us who lack a certain element usually have a difficult time relating to and naturally expressing that element. For example, if you have little or none of the fire element in your birthchart, you may find it difficult to be spontaneous and express spirit or enthusiasm.

Healing requires our conscious effort to restore our own natural balance. Beyond that, it requires bringing all of the elements, whether we have natural energy for them or not, into harmony.

Those who chose birth patterns with a natural distribution of fire, earth, air, and water may have a bit of an edge, but only a slight edge. There may be a more clearly defined framework to support the return to the original self. However, whether you have an equal natural distribution of the elements in your makeup or lots of variation, as the pattern of your life unfolds, your birthchart pattern of elements shifts and changes. The heavenly bodies are in constant motion. The interrelationship of the planets in the sky right now with the pattern of planets in your unique birthchart affects, sometimes profoundly, your original elemental makeup.

Whether you have an equal natural distribution of the elements in your chart or a preponderance or lack of certain elements, the natural unfolding of your pattern in relation to the impact of the current position of planets puts emphasis on certain aspects of your life's expression and experience. Planetary emphasis on the water element in your chart will, through both internal experience and external circumstances, sometimes prompt, sometimes impel you, to deal with your emotions and feelings. Emphasis on the earth element in your nature brings internal and external promptings telling you to take care of your physical dimension, your body. Sometimes this is expressed through health issues or the need for you to become aware of and pay attention to your body's needs.

How you respond to the promptings of the universe is up to you. I have always had a great respect and appreciation for the symbolic language of astrology. The birthchart and the current pattern in the sky offer great insight into personal potential for growth and wholeness. The astrological approach can identify the need for individual healing. It can reflect and suggest the areas in most need of healing. Astrology is a valuable tool; yet it is only a tool. Astrology cannot, in itself, heal you. That takes conscious awareness and your commitment to healing according to the unfolding of your unique life pattern.

Another view of the birthchart shows an individual's natural feminine and masculine energy. Irrespective of our female or male anatomy, we each have both feminine and masculine energy in our makeup. Some years ago, the trend among astrologers was to change the terminology to negative and positive energy. The feminine energy, of course, got the negative pole since we are considered the receptive diodes. I do not buy that at all. I also believe the change in terminology reflected some deep-seated homophobia rather than political correctness. In any case, I affirm both my female and male energies and proudly refer to them as such.

The ten planets, including the sun and moon, operate in either a feminine or masculine mode. Within each of us is a mix of these energies vying for expression. Our culture has had an amazing impact on our ability to feel comfortable with the natural energies of our birth patterns.

As women become more visible and valued in our

society, we are beginning to hear the value of men getting in touch with their feminine side. Male privilege may discourage women from getting in touch with their masculine side but many women know better. Individually, it is only when we are able to give expression to the mix of both energies that we can experience balance and wholeness. Because almost everywhere on earth feminine energy has been suppressed, *the greatest potential for global harmony lies first in the worldwide healing of feminine energy.*

Our culture devalues feelings and the display of emotion. Girls are not supposed to get angry. Boys are not supposed to cry and, for that matter, girls are not supposed to cry either. Emotions are supposed to be held in check or displayed in private. Our mass suppression of feelings has begun to erupt everywhere. Cultural suppression of anger has turned into hostility which has exploded into a crisis of abuse and violence. Both women and men suffer from the mass suppression of emotions, the feminine energy. The first, and most important, need we have as a society right now is the need for emotional healing.

I spent many years, sometimes full-time, sometimes part-time, as an activist in the women's movement. We lobbied, picketed, conducted speakouts on important issues to women, leafletted, phonebanked, marched on Washington, marched on Albany, N.Y., held meetings, held meetings to plan meetings, staffed crisis lines, formed support groups, got media attention, and got Washington's attention. There is no question that the women's movement to date has made important changes for women. Sometimes it has been two steps forward and one back. Sometimes it has been one step forward and two back. Sometimes it appears that the more things change, the more they stay the same. But, over the course of the years since my awareness of the women's movement, concrete and tangible changes have been made. There have also been positive changes in the perception of women and women's value in our society.

I did, however, begin to examine the need for cultural emotional healing in terms of the women's movement. It is mostly the women's movement where I have had direct experience, but I believe this applies to other social justice movements as well.

My specific experience is with NOW, the National Organization for Women. I became a member in the nineteen-seventies, early in the organization's history. I became an activist in the mid-nineteen-eighties. From ninety-ninety-one until the beginning of nineteen-ninety-five, almost every aspect of my life had become inextricably linked to the National Organization for Women. I gave it my best and my all; and I take full responsibility for my burnout.

Months later, in the midst of my own emotional healing, I began to examine my experience with the women's movement. The media, especially the print media, put the women's movement under attack in recent years. It was common to read in a newspaper or magazine that the women's movement was dying, or worse, the movement was dead. Inside the movement we all agreed this was a media ploy; we would have to do more to get more attention and better press coverage. We simply had to do more, be more visible, and rock more boats.

A lot of the organization's activists have been activists for a long time and have given well past the point where it hurts. Just when we needed new energy and perspective, potential activists, the young feminists, were turning a deaf ear to the movement. Why were we not able to enlist the support of young women, many of whose mothers had worked so long and hard to make strides for them? Didn't these young women, especially those on college campuses, appreciate all we older feminists had done for them?

That is the problem. We have done it for them. We have, through our organization, created a power imbalance and a rescuer/victim mentality.

For three years I ran a statewide NOW office and was a local chapter president for two years. Because of the organization's high visibility, we got many calls from women in various kinds of crisis situations. Most often we were called as a last resort, after every other avenue had been pursued. More often than not the call came from a woman who was not nor had ever been a member but believed that, since NOW is a women's organization, we should be interested in her plight.

Looking back, it is amusing to see what a predicament I had put myself in. I was the classic rescuer who prided herself on helping others, fixing things, and making it better; and I was constantly faced with last resort calls from women in impossible situations who expected me to make it better and fix it. At the time, of course, it was a tremendous source of frustration. I spent more energy that I care to admit wrestling with my dilemma. It was a factor that led to my sense of powerlessness and burnout and a theme that repeated itself, over and over, in my life crisis.

I also saw this pattern and its counterpart, the victim, reflected in my organization. The National Organization for Women, in many ways, is perceived as the organization that can fight for and solve all the societal problems faced by today's woman. In many ways, NOW encourages that perception by actually trying to do it all; giving attention to almost any issue that affects women; and, encouraging its members to take united action in a dizzying array of activities. Often "encouraging" is "guilt tripping" and the organization, rife with Earth Mother-rescuer types, is suffering badly from burnout.

Burned-out leaders and activists are cast aside, often treated like worn-out "combat" boots. The rescuer mentality is so strong that, even some of the burn out victims do not seem to know when to stop. The culture of the organization discourages stopping. The message to the rescuers is "If we don't do it (all for them), who will?" Inside the movement, behind closed doors, we ask, "Why do we treat our leaders and activists so badly?"

Not all of the leadership of NOW are rescuers. The organization has its share of political opportunists in highly visible positions. While it would be easy to cite specific examples, this is a book about healing, not an exposé of NOW's leadership. The predominant culture of the organization is that of the superwoman who can and should do it all for womankind. Some women keep going out of guilt and some out of loyalty, both are notions that can get us in a lot of trouble. Guilt and loyalty keep us in blinders, unable to clearly see our inability to "fix" others' problems.

The women's movement has made much progress over the past three decades. I believe, however, that unless the organizations that shape the movement change, the women's movement, as such, has reached a point of diminishing returns.

The National Organization for Women, the most influential organization in the women's movement, is based on a male hierarchal model. In many ways it is a mirror reflection of the very societal structures the organization wants to change. Much of NOW's activity, or "actions", are reactions. The reactions are, more often than not, carried out as protest and resistance, accompanied by a lot of anger and outrage.

I have come to see the truth in the statement, "What you resist persists"; and how that has operated in my past. Putting effort and energy into what you do not want binds it to you. The most damaging effect of resisting what you do not want is that you give your power over to the people and things you are resisting. I see this on a larger scale in the women's movement. Time and again, in fighting for women's rights, far too much attention is paid to "the other side" and what we do not want. This all too often results in the media spotlight being directed at "the opposition".

A couple of years ago NOW sponsored a Pro-Choice Rally in Washington, D.C. Pro-Choice supporters turned out over a million strong. A mere handful of anti-choice protestors huddled together with huge anti-choice picket signs. Guess who got equal television coverage? The media does seem to apply its own interpretation to karmic balance.

In addition to over a million of us "sending a message to Washington", we gave a lot of power away. And, in making our pilgrimage to Washington, we each, unknowingly, acknowledged that those in Washington, the seat of the nation's power, call the shots for women's reproductive rights.

For twenty years, I was a corporate executive and I understand corporate power structures. NOW, a male modeled structure is what is referred to as a top-down organization; the power is at the top and runs down to the bottom, the general membership. Within the organization, decision making occurs on a very hierarcal structure. The real power resides at the top and is passed down.

Many feminists believe our organizations should be bottom-up, that is, the power from the general membership should be passed up to the top. But the real problem is it is still a male model as long as there is a bottom and top level.

Consensus decision making, where everyone's voice is taken into consideration, is the most equitable and, in fact, most natural approach for many women. Unfortunately, consensus decision making is time consuming and inefficient in groups involving large numbers.

I have great respect for the past contributions made by my sisters in NOW. I have great respect for my own contributions to this organization. I stated earlier that, although my experience is with the women's movement, NOW in particular; I believe my realizations apply to other social movements as well.

In 1992, I was one of the Buffalo United for Choice organizers that kept Operation Rescue from shutting down clinics during their Spring of Life campaign.

Through sheer numbers on our side, the pro-choice majority in Buffalo won a major victory through non-violent resistance. Both sides got major national media attention; but no one in the media could deny that the well-organized pro-choice defense strategy of non-violent resistance struck a major blow to the anti-choice movement nationwide.

The long-term effect of the major victory in Buffalo, and subsequent similar victories in other cities, was, however, not so positive. The energy of resistance built up and exploded in violence and the killing of dedicated healthcare professionals.

I now believe the sooner abortion rights are legislated away, the sooner we women will have the opportunity to take back our personal and collective power to provide for our own reproductive healthcare. Once abortion rights are no longer a government and legislative issue; even if abortion becomes illegal, women will find caring and appropriate ways to handle their own reproductive healthcare. Women took care of themselves in the past, as many older women have disclosed. Knowledge and procedures were passed from woman-to-woman, sometimes from generation-to-generation. The times were different and attitudes were different, but there were still strong women who did what they had to do. There were still wise women, "medicine women", who shared their knowledge of herbs and abortion procedures.

Today there are women's self-help healthcare groups and collectives that operate in various parts of the country. For the most part, they operate quietly and efficiently, ready for the time when the gov-

ernment no longer has control of women's reproductive healthcare.

Social and political activist organizations are caught
in the resist/persist trap, often resulting in even more of
what is not wanted. My own organization, NOW, suffers
from the creation of the rescuer/victim mentality and I
see this same phenomena in other activist organizations
like the Lesbian and Gay Rights Movement.

The issue is power. Although the social justice
movements create the perception of power, sometimes
by the sheer number of members, the clout is in the
hands of a few who must, through protest and resistance, give the power over to "the other side". There is
no real power, only perceived power. Real power can
only come from empowered members, individuals who
are each self-empowered and united for something positive. Inherent in the male hierarcal structure adopted by
many organizations is discouragement of self-empowerment and individualism. The organizations are top-heavy
with bureaucrats who have learned to manipulate the
heirarchal power to their own advantage.

If, because of their very nature, our social and political activist organizations, cannot change and are destined
to become ineffective, how do we create the kind of
change necessary to move us into a society where each
individual is valued and respected? What do we do?

Right now the most important need is individual
emotional healing. Emotion is the feminine energy in
each of us. Women, as the clearest expression of the
feminine energy, are powerful nurturers and caregivers.
Our male dominated and hierarchic culture has done
an excellent job convincing women that there is only value

in our nurturing and caregiving when it is given to others. Much in our culture encourages us to give our power away when self-empowerment is the only real power.

The only empowering way for women is the way of self-empowerment and self-direction. The female energy is the creative energy. Individually and collectively, we must stop giving our power over to others. Once we heal ourselves, especially our own female emotional energy, we heal the universe.

Before there can be a society of self-empowered individuals, major emotional healing has to occur. It can only happen one-by-one but the collective effect will have a major impact. Within the women's movement, individual women must begin to recognize the need for healing and commit to their individual self-empowerment. As more and more women involve themselves in the healing process, the power of the healing energy will have a major impact on all of society.

Imagine what would happen if we just stopped our political activism, protest, and resistance. Imagine what would happen if we, individually and collectively, simply stepped up and claimed what is ours?

Terry Cole Whittaker, in her book, *Love and Power in a World Without Limits*, talks about "disappearing" things. She explains that when we react to something or act in opposition to it, we actually give our power over to it. We perpetuate an enemy by believing there is an enemy and affirming it. We further empower our enemies by believing they can control or limit us in some way. To 'disappear' something give your attention to what you want, instead of what you don't want. Keep your focus forward and on the positive instead of backward and on the negative.

Stopping is the first step. By stopping we create breathing room and a space for healing to begin. Breath and Spirit come from the same root meaning. To create breathing room, to breathe, we create spiritual energy and align with all of Universal Energy. This is a powerful act. Our very breathing is a powerful act. Each time we take a breath we align with spiritual energy.

We need to stop giving our power over to our government and our institutions. This does not necessarily mean pulling out of the system. It does mean we stop putting our precious time and energy into perpetuating what we want to change, such as our elective political system.

The next step is to move forward. Each of us must move toward what we want in our lives and proudly claim what is ours. This may mean replacing parts of our culture that have no place for us because their very nature is exclusively male energy. It may also mean establishing alternate institutions, such as businesses, that are in tune with female energy. For each woman, individually, stepping forward may have a slightly different meaning. We have to respect each other. We have to respect individualism. As we claim and assert what is ours, the expression of our own self-esteem commands respect from others. When one woman steps up and claims what is hers, we all move forward.

The universe is constantly changing. In fact, the only certainty in the universe is change. As a reflection of the universe, you are constantly changing. This change is the internal natural impulse for growth. It is our impulse for achieving balance. Your commitment to your own healing is a powerful acknowledgment of your own natural impulses. To embrace the growth and change inherent in your life pattern is to celebrate your uniqueness and integrity.

Everything in the universe is interconnected, each of us to each other. What we do to ourselves has an effect on everyone else. This also applies on a personal level to the elements. Personal healing involves fire, earth, air, and water. Spirit, body, mind, and emotions are interrelated. Whatever you do to affect a personal healing in one area, will have a positive impact on all other areas. For example, if you decide to pay attention to your body, you may decide to get more exercise, improve your nutrition, or take some other steps that improve your health.

The result of these healing actions is that you feel better. Take a look at the components of feeling better. Because you have taken some physical healing actions, your attitude (mind) is positive, you feel (emotion) better about yourself, and you are enthusiastic and energetic (spirit). Feeling better actually means experiencing yourself more fully as yourself. As you identify and take action to heal individual aspects of yourself, realize that what you do for one aspect of yourself positively affects all of you. This is healing for balance. It is healing for wholeness. It is recognizing your personal power to restore your own unique well-being.

The outcome of healing is balance and wholeness which results in experiencing personal power — self-esteem. When you operate out of self-esteem you are then able to take personal responsibility for the direction of your own life path.

Global Healing

We can heal our planet, bring about a restoration of elemental balance resulting in peace and harmony, by the conscious commitment on the part of individuals to heal themselves. Because we are all connected in the Great Cosmic Web, one person's healing affects everyone else's healing.

Karma is the natural law of balance. In the long view, over time, everything in the Universe comes into balance. It is sometimes difficult for us to understand karma because of the human approach to time. We understand time in components; past, present, and future. But time is a human construct. The Universe is not limited by the notion of time. Karma operates perfectly, creating perfect balance, in a timeless framework.

Although the human mind, because of our orientation to the notion of time, cannot continuously grasp the timelessness of the Universe, we can, from time to time, experience a glimpse of knowing. Your willingness to let go of the human notion of time, even if for a brief moment, will cause a shift in consciousness. It is the conscious shift you create that enables you to participate in the energy of karmic balance and achieve a great healing for yourself.

This is a time of great personal and planetary potential. On January 16, 1995 Pluto made its introductory move into Sagittarius. Although Pluto went back into Scorpio for a last bit of cleanup, in November 1995, Pluto moves into Sagittarius for a long stay (until 2008). Pluto, in its own sign of Scorpio since the early eighties, uncovered and exposed much abuse, decay, and turmoil. Individuals with strong Pluto signatures in their charts were especially affected.

Pluto in Sagittarius offers the possibility of a great healing for the planet. Those who have learned to use Pluto's personal magic and transformative power for themselves, will be called to share their healing power. From January to November 1995, Pluto rocked back into Scorpio for a final time. Many healers, especially those with a twelfth house/ Pisces/Neptune chart emphasis and a Pluto/Scorpio/eighth house chart emphasis, experienced death, loss, and letting go. With this comes the opportunity for tremendous personal healing. It is a time of choosing conscious transformation. It is a time of accepting being chosen for the healing work that must be shared when Pluto's potential unfolds in Sagittarius.

The kind of healing work that must be done is defined only in terms of that which promotes wholeness and completeness. Healing involves the responsible use of positive personal energy and power. Healers must work in many different areas. Besides those in the traditional healing and helping professions, healers must work within business and industry, institutions, and political arenas.

Because healers are identified astrologically by the twelfth house/Pisces/Neptune and Pluto/Scorpio/eighth house chart emphasis, it is important to understand these patterns. Pluto in the twelfth house is especially indicative of healers. Those with a twelfth house Pluto are particularly affected by the current Pluto Scorpio-Sagittarius dance.

The astrological twelfth house is the accumulation of all the energies from the entire circle of houses. It is the last, the highest, and the most misunderstood house of the chart. It is the unconscious and the superconscious. This house is the alpha and omega. In the twelfth house resides the potential for personal destruction and dissolution. The potential for recreation, rebirth and reincarnation exists within the twelfth house also. And in the twelfth house lies the secret to personal power, magic and transformation.

The twelfth house is the bridge from the human and physical to the psychic and spiritual. It bridges personal and collective energies. The twelfth house exists in a psychic personal dimension and attracts and collects energies from other chart houses or life areas. Thus, the twelfth house is a grand accumulation of individual psychic treasures as well as individual psychic trash.

The twelfth house is the house of the collective unconscious, so the accumulation may include others' psychic garbage also. Any planet in the twelfth house is vitally important as it operates in very powerful, often uncontrollable, ways.

Pluto, is the smallest, yet most powerful, planet. Although a neutral energy until activated, Pluto carries the greatest potential for personal destruction and the greatest potential for personal transformation. It is the great destroyer and the great rebuilder. It represents the endings in which there are always new beginnings.

Symbolically, Pluto, in its mundane form, is the scorpion. In its spiritual form, Pluto is the eagle. In the threefold god of eastern philosophy, Brahma is the creator, Vishnu, the preserver and Shiva, the destroyer. Pluto is Shiva, the destroyer, who keeps the world in a constant state of change. Through the music and magic of Shiva/Pluto, transformation is an ever present possibility.

Pluto is two-faced. One face is death, loss, devastation and despair. The other face is magic, healing and transformation. Pluto exposes the dark side, the underworld and the depths of the unconscious. It strips away, often in brutal and savage ways, everything in its path. It ensures that the way to transformation is clear. Pluto then offers a glimpse of transformation, the way of the eagle, and an opportunity to reach out and choose it.

The call of Pluto is a call for healers to heal themselves. As healers commit to personal transformation, the personal healing that occurs will result in a great outpouring of healing energy for the planet.

It takes but a handful of us to affect great change for our planet. Ernest Holmes, a great spiritual teacher and founder of the Science of Mind philosophy in 1927, said, "A little bit of leaven leavens the whole lump." A pinch of yeast raises the whole loaf. A committed band of conscious individuals heals the whole planet.

Effective Healing Approaches ————

Many effective healing approaches are included in this section. You do not have to do them all to get the benefit of personal healing. In fact, you do not have to adopt any of them; but they are, individually and collectively, highly effective. The truth is, your healing begins once you acknowledge your need and commit to being open to accepting healing energy.

The name of this wonderful game is getting in touch with yourself and following the healing path that feels right for you. The way the game is played is that you get to create your own space of healing and select your own game pieces — your own healing approaches. It is called being kind to yourself and accepting your own pace and natural flow.

You may choose to do " speed healing" and use as many healing approaches as possible. Healing occurs on many levels and in many layers. It can be helpful to involve yourself in as many different approaches to healing as possible at the same time. Keep in mind, though, the idea of healing is not to overwork yourself; but to take it easy and learn to listen to yourself.

The whole point of healing is recuperation and restoration of your original self.

Most of us have become so used to the effort and struggle in our lives that we, at first, believe we have to work at this, too. Many of us have been on the path of self-discovery and self-actualization for many years. Major life transitions and personal crises can have a double whammy effect. The reality of what has happened to your world is a major shock to your spiritual, mental, emotional, and physical makeup. On top of this, there is a tendency to beat yourself up when you think about all the conscious self-development energy you have already expended in the past. You think you should be able to control or rise above your crisis circumstances. How could this have happened to you?

Time for a reality check. No one's efforts at self-growth and self-actualization are ever wasted or for naught. Your circumstances are just your circumstances, part of your unique life path. You chose this life, then forgot why you did it. There is, however, an overall point to it all, even if you cannot see it. There is a power greater than you that knows the game plan. That power is part of your makeup also. All you need to do is surrender to your personal power, your piece of the Universal Energy web. Step into the flow of your life; trust and relax.

Healing is not necessarily a growth experience in that it does not have to be difficult or effort-intensive. The only test is your own test. How good do you feel? How "together" do you feel? How much love and appreciation do you have for yourself?

Here, then, is my list of healing approaches. Try

one. Try them all. Pick the ones that seem natural to you at first; then, be adventurous, and try the others. Some of these approaches may seem a little risky at first. Some of them may seem threatening. Yet these may be the very approaches that will have the most healing effect on you. Many of us on a healing trip were brought here courtesy of a complete breakdown in our lives. When you have the opportunity to recreate your life, there's no better time to fly in the face of all your fears and leap into the promise of healing. For those of you who have a chance to choose healing as a preventive measure before crisis shakes your roots, leap into the promise of healing with all your might now. You will not prevent the crisis that may be inherent in your life pattern; but you will get to experience whatever your life has in store for you from a healthier and more balanced perspective.

Self-Help and Inspirational Books

Read all the inspirational, spiritual, and motivational books you can get into your hands. Fill your mind with positive thoughts and ideas. Feed your head healthy mental food. If there were books that made powerful impressions on you before, reread them. Remember, we forget, and it is all right to forget. In fact, it is perfectly human. Allow your healing space to be a refresher course and take what was best from your past and give it another review. Chances are, if you found it helpful before, it will be healing and helpful again.

Meditation

Almost every religion, philosophy, and New Age practice describes a specific approach to meditation from the necessity of making your mind a blank screen to holding one thought in your mind for a specific amount of time. Some religions equate prayer with meditation while others include reflective reading. There is a huge amount of information available on the proper way to meditate. Studying this information can give you plenty of data for lively discussion and debate. Yet, it is my experience, that there is only one right way to meditate and that is the way that works for you.

The whole point of meditation is to allow focus and flow to come into your mind. Whatever comes easily to you is your right way to meditate. You might try making your mind a blank screen and holding it for a certain amount of time. I personally believe this requires a lifetime of real effort and struggle but maybe it will work for you. You might try just sitting with your eyes closed, breathing deeply, and holding a positive thought or question in your mind. You might be more comfortable keeping your eyes open and directing your attention on a scene or picture. I have set my computer to display an array of floating stars. When I cannot do my meditation outdoors in the sunshine or under the night sky, the high-tech way is very effective for me.

You might try meditative reading. *The Woman's Book of Courage by* Sue Patton Thoele was there for me at the beginning of my journey out of darkness into healing when I needed to find the most courage to break out of my circumstances. There have been other wonderful books of meditative readings along my path and I am very grateful for them all. I have found the books that offer daily calendar readings to be uncannily appropriate. Then I remember that nothing in this universe happens by chance.

Affirmations

Affirmations are positive statements, that, when repeated over and over, actually reinvigorate and restore well-being. There is great healing power in the use of affirmations. Your thoughts are energy. By affirming, for example, "I am in balance with my true self" and repeating this statement over and over, you actually shape your mental energy. You have the power to shape your own mind. Since all energy is interconnected, even your thought energy, your ability to shape your own thought has a far-reaching influence. Through simple, positive affirmations you have the power to generate positive energy both within and outside your physical self.

There is also great power in the energy of your voice. When affirmations are spoken and repeated aloud, you can double the impact. Affirmations that are "I" statements like "I am whole and centered" or "I love myself and the Goddess within me", when stated in front of a mirror have almost a magical effect. Look into your own eyes and deep within yourself, repeat your affirmation over and over until you actually feel the powerful energy of your words.

At first, you may feel like you are merely trying to convince yourself; but keep at it. State your affirmations with enthusiasm until you experience a positive shift.

Start with an affirmation that feels right for you. Affirmations that are short, simple, and begin with "I" statements are the most immediately effective. "I am happy and healthy," when repeated with enthusiasm, creates amazing healing vibrations.

Most of us talk to ourselves. We say we do it because who else will listen? The truth is, who better to listen? The energy of our self-talk has a powerful influence on our overall well-being. Those of us embarrassed about talking to ourselves now have a way to make it legitimate — by speaking affirmations.

Action

There are some who claim that healing is a natural process that occurs after shock and trauma and nothing is required of a person other than to just be. We have all heard the phrase, "Let nature take its course." The idea is a good one. The problem is that most of us have put so much of ourselves in the way of nature taking its course. We have to clear away a lot of mental, physical, spiritual, and emotional debris before we can open ourselves to healing and "letting nature take its course".

Reading self-help books, meditating, and speaking affirmations are positive healing approaches. However, healing yourself for long-term and lasting effects requires your active participation. Healing requires action and movement. It requires practical application. When you combine mental and emotional healing approaches with physical action, you create a strong energy force of personal power. You can read every self-help book available and get mental healing; but your overall healing will probably be limited.

When you involve your physical self through action and movement you quickly multiply the effects of healing. Walking, running, dancing, exercising, or any movement that feels good to you is helpful. Take action that gives you a sense of flow and momentum. The object of the game of your healing is to restore wholeness and balance. Give equal time to your physical self and enjoy some physical activity every day.

Ritual

Ritual is the performance of certain actions that enable us to focus, and transform, our spirits. Ritual differs from routine in that it takes into account the potential power of our personal spiritual energy. Ritual has the power to transcend time. Through rituals we can reestablish our connection to old and sacred traditions.

For seven years, I was a member of a women's spirituality circle, a coven. Almost from the beginning, we developed a web of support and caring that became very precious to each of us. I will always value that wonderful experience. Together, we reestablished our natural connection with the Ancient Mother, the Goddess in her many forms. I, and many of my coven sisters, had become disillusioned with many of our cultural and religious traditions. Together, we explored and came to appreciate the value of Goddess-centered ritual and tradition.

Many rituals transcend religion and philosophy and continue to offer great healing potential. Lighting candles and burning incense help us create an atmosphere for healing. Candles and meditation are an especially powerful healing combination. My favorite form of ritual is chanting, the ancient version of modern affirmation. I am a lover of music so I like to sing my chants. Singing chants while walking is a healing experience I highly recommend. Find a local playground and let your inner child swing while chanting, "Body, mind, feelings, and spirit." This is a wonderful and exhilarating way to get all yourself in balance.

Feeling Your Feelings

Daily life involves our feelings. When daily life is colored by major life changes, our feelings are intensified. There is no area in greater need of healing than our emotional selves. The feminine energy in all of us has been suppressed by our culture for far too long and the effects are far too damaging to deny any longer.

It is impossible to experience wholeness without emotional healing. Major life transitions elicit a range of intense feelings from sadness, loss, grief, hurt, and anger to relief, joy, and contentment. During many life changes, the full range of feelings can surface and erupt almost simultaneously. This is an extremely important time to sort out and accept all your feelings. Feelings are an important aspect of yourself, as important as the physical, mental, and spiritual dimensions. And, while feelings are an important aspect of your total self that need equal treatment, feelings are just feelings. Your emotions are an important part of you and they are but a part of you.

As a natural part of your self-expression, it is okay to cry. In fact, it is more than okay to cry; it is vital. Tears are necessary and important for healing. Suppressing tears blocks the full flow of healing energy.

It is also vitally important to laugh which has a similar release effect to crying. Just as we have societal taboos against crying, we also have taboos against laughing, especially in life circumstances involving death and loss.

Near the first anniversary of my mother's death, my sister and I attended a birthday party for my mother's closest friend. All my mother's lifelong circle of friends were there, as well as family friends. Initially our socializing was sprinkled with comments about missing her. We were all sensitive to the fact that it had been just a year since she died. But, soon, we got down to celebrating her life and, as only her dear friends could do, "telling on her". My sister and I got to hear the retelling of many stories my mother had told us so many times. This time we heard them from her friends' point of view. I remember two hours of uproarious laughter as, one after another, the old stories were told. My mother's presence was very real that evening. She loved to laugh; we all laughed with her; and we shared some very important healing energy.

Tears and laughter are powerful healing experiences. It is important to capture these feelings as they come up and let yourself fully experience them. Many of us have years of pent up emotions that deserve our gentle acceptance and as much time as it takes to clear all the blocked channels.

By far, the emotion on which society has placed the strongest taboo is anger. I believe that anger is the most important feeling to feel because we have all been denied our anger for so long. Blocked anger is toxic to ourselves and others. Many of us go through most of our lives trying so hard not to be angry that we completely lose touch with our anger. Anger does not go away. Ignore it, stuff it away, repress it, do not admit it, do not handle it. Then, all of a sudden, our out-of-control anger is the only thing that is running the show and we do not even know it.

During the summer of my healing, I came to terms with the role anger had played in my life. Throughout my life I saw myself as an angry person. Others saw me as a nice person. My mother was my role model for angry people. She did the best she could with her anger and I do not blame her for my own anger. I did learn a lot from her, though, about repressing and misdirecting anger. I learned a lot from her about not being entitled to your own anger. I learned how to make excuses for others. I can honestly say I became an expert at this. Time after time, once I got myself to calm down, a trick that became harder and harder over the years, I would find a way to excuse and "write it off". I also became an expert at self-deceit! Though I had done all the things to learn to be a properly assertive person in the outside world, my childhood patterns still ran my personal life.

I have always considered myself a recovering Catholic. I "dropped out" of going to Mass at the age of fifteen but I still had two more years in a Catholic high school to contend with. I am not sure how well I escaped the messages of the last two years of high school, but, in doing my early childhood healing work, I realize most of the job was done on me by about ten years old. I know different people take different messages from their early religious training. I know I took some real doosies. For many years I have said that I thought one thing the Catholic Church does better than any other religion is get them while they are young. The Roman Catholic approach is early indoctrination. By the time children reach the age of seven or so, they have had an encapsulated version of all the religion's teachings. By the "age of reason" we were told not to bother to reason.

Like many recovering Catholics, I have had a good time with Catholic humor. All the jokes and laughs about growing up Catholic provide a kind of pressure valve for a lot of frustration and anger. At fifteen, I combined this humor with my own brand of wit and cynicism and became fairly well known for my irreverence. I can be irreverent about almost anything. My irreverence does have a tendency to throw those folks who have cast me as a nice person. I am sure that is one of the reasons I use my irreverent streak so much.

The messages of the Catholic church that hooked me at a very early age were the notions of sacrifice and martyrdom. How those saints, especially the women, were personified as heroic victims. My favorite was, and still is, Joan of Arc, who heroically saved her town, then was burned at the stake for her efforts. I have huge amounts of anger at the Catholic Church for dishing out that bowl of gruel especially, when, at such an early age, I slurped it up and asked for more.

For 24 years I had been with a partner who was angry. Our inability to identify, express, and deal with anger, mostly the passive-aggressive kind, was a factor that lead to a very rough ending. I also saw that my life in recent years had become filled with angry people, especially angry women. Unresolved anger is toxic.

I have had a passion for music all my life. I grew up with constant music. My grandmother and her sister sang and played piano in local clubs during the nineteen-twenties. My mother sang with local Big Band groups in the forties. Even though my father left when I was age nine, I remember that he had a nice singing voice also. My childhood was filled with music, mostly pop music. We all sang and, as I remember it, we sang just about everywhere. From today's perspective, my family had its dysfunctional aspects, but I remember a childhood filled with a good amount of laughter and lots of singing.

Since the beginning of my breakup, the breakout phase, music had become a torture for me. At first, being a lifelong music lover, I thought my hypersensitivity had to do with my habit of attaching my own experiences to music.

Suddenly everything I listened to had a painful emotional impact. I had been used to having background music in my office; I played the radio or tapes in my car; and, I have always had my own internal Musak system in my head. In fact, I have been so attuned to music over the years that I got into the habit of stopping to see what tune was running in my head as a way of "checking in" to see what was going on with me. Now everything I "checked into" was pain. Easy Listening was anything but easy. Golden Oldies were anything but golden.

Carol King's *Tapestry* album was a favorite at the beginning of our relationship. In early 1995, I started to hear the album everywhere. Every time I went to the supermarket, one of the cuts from that album would shoot out of the sound system straight into my breaking heart. I actually had an incident that involved a young checkout clerk, a finicky cash register, "You've Got a Friend," and me in tears. I won't get into the specifics. You probably get the connections.

I started to develop a phobia about supermarkets. Actually, it went back to the end of nineteen-ninety-three when my mother died. It seemed I often had to decide whether to abandon my cart somewhere in the middle of the store. The only thing that kept me going was the thought that I would have to come back and start over. Piped in music can be hard on a captive audience.

As I was beginning to get paranoid about the Carol King *Tapestry* album and the fact that I heard cuts from it everywhere, I realized that the album was twenty-five years old. It was getting a lot of air play because of its 25th anniversary. Of course, realizing that explained why I was hearing the album all the time and, in many ways, just made it all worse.

I tried to suffer through the music for awhile. As I started to pay attention to lyrics and began to examine the messages, I realized the profound effect music had had on my entire life. Because of my lifelong connection and exposure to music, my values, ideals, and attitudes were greatly shaped by music.

Around the time I was coming to the conclusion that most music was unhealthy for me, the Barbra Streisand 1994 Concert album arrived in the mail. I had forgotten I ordered it. I decided to take the time to listen to it once, experience all the pain of the memories, and treat it as a gift for my healing. The gift, indeed, contained a special treasure. When I heard Barbra Streisand say that she no longer wanted to sing "victim" songs, major bells went off in my head. "Of course," I thought, "that was a big part of what was wrong with the music I had always listened to." Then I realized that that was only part of it; the other part was "rescuer" songs.

As I started to pay even more attention to lyrics, I saw how much of it is based on the victim-rescuer connection. In fact, love, the most common theme in all music, is tragically misstated and misrepresented.

Much of the music, especially popular music, reflects the unhealthy attitudes of our culture. Pain, suffering, giving all to get love, making someone else happy, whole or worthwhile do not promote or support healing. The messages of much of popular culture's music keeps us stuck in an endless cycle of self-denial and destruction. Popular music may be an expression of common emotions, but the messages about common attitudes are unhealthy.

I do not indiscriminately listen to the radio in my office or car. I monitor the Muzak in my head these days. If it's negative message music, I switch it off. I still have a passion for music — healthy, positive music.

We are an angry people. My experience in the women's movement helped me see how unresolved anger gets confused and misapplied as power. The increasing violence in our society is a reflection of deep-seated and misplaced anger.

It is time to recognize and own your anger. There are many available books on the subject. There is a lot of available professional help. Take the time to explore your anger, especially past and early childhood anger. Your anger is an important part of you. Once you identify it, see the value it has for you. It can be an important key to how you recreate your world. Anger transformed into positive action can change your world.

It really is time for a Great Healing. I do believe that can happen. In fact, it has already started by individuals around the globe making the commitment to personal healing and transformation. The only way to have a Great Healing, a global healing, is through a one-by-one commitment. When you make a commitment to live in love, through your connectedness to everyone else, you affect the whole. We can change from an angry people to a loving people.

Getting In Touch With Your Body

It is so easy to get out of touch with your body and so important to get back in touch. The body is a won-

derful container and connector of all the other personal energies — spirit, emotion, and mind. Because
of the interconnectedness of your earth, air, fire, and
water energies, any attention you pay to healing your body
immediately affects your mind, emotions, and spirit, also.

The first thing to do is to begin to listen, really
listen, to your body. Where are you holding stress? What
hurts? What aches? Which parts of your body are longing for some attention? In the stillness you create in
meditation or reflective quiet, you can not only ask
your body questions, but you can also get answers. If
you locate an area of your body that aches or hurts,
talk to it and ask that part what it needs. Center on
your body as a whole and ask what your body needs to
feel more balanced and alive.

At first, this is often hard to do, especially during
very stressful times, because many of us have gotten
very out of touch with our physical sense of balance.
Many of the messages we get from outside us encourage us to ignore, or, at least, mask, our bodies' signals.
We snuff out our warning indicators with pills, potions,
and poisonous substances.

Early in my breakout phase, I realized that my body,
my physical self, was, and had been, about ten steps
ahead of the rest of me. Intense physical pain accompanied my psychological pain. I began to listen and I
began to take some healing action. Walking, fresh air
exercise, and swinging on the local playground swings
helped me recover a sense of balance and I needed, in
fact, craved, that regimen daily.

Massage therapy was wonderful also. During one
of my early sessions, a great deal of my physical and

emotional pain surfaced. My therapist helped me identify the physical source of the pain. I experienced and told her that my heart was in pieces and I did not feel I could hold the pieces together any longer. I learned that I could talk to my heart and make it healthy again.

The range of physical healing approaches is broad and includes everything from formal physical programs and therapies to informal exercise and activities. The only important thing is to begin to listen to your body, find out what it needs, and take some action.

Your physical energy heals through physical, sensual, and sexual activity. Pay attention. Respect what your body tells you. The moment you begin to listen and commit to your body's healing, you begin to shift all of your energy back into its natural balance and wholeness.

Identifying Your Inner Selves

A highly effective approach to healing is getting in touch with your inner selves. We all have selves within ourselves. Some of our inner selves dominate us. Some of our inner selves operate behind the scenes. Many of us have parts of ourselves, inner selves, that we have cut off or disowned.

Yet, we cannot separate ourselves from ourselves. Our hidden selves or shadow selves press for attention, often causing us to act out or behave inappropriately. The selves we allow to dominate us often run out of control. Many of us need to rediscover our inner selves and figure out how the gang can become a team.

We all have an inner child. Our inner child is our first self, our original self, and our child self is completely innocent. We carry our inner child with us throughout our lives. Through our life's journey many of us either disown or become alienated from our inner child.

We also have other selves within us. We have an inner critic who begs, pleads, and nags. We have an adolescent who carries our dreams and visions of youth. We have an inner parent who nurtures and protects us. And we have a guide or psychic.

Identifying your inner selves takes a little time. We have all become accustomed to ignoring ourselves. Take some time to listen to yourself. Listen to your inner voices and messages. Ask yourself who is speaking, then listen again. After awhile, you will get an answer.

Be kind and gentle with yourself. Each of your inner selves is a special and precious part of you. As you identify your inner selves, begin an internal dialogue. Tell them you understand they have the need for expression and attention. Make any apologies you need to make.

Along with a commitment to healing, I made a commitment to be willing to understand myself, all of myself, as many aspects and layers as possible. Metaphysically, when you agree to be willing to something, your willingness melts away resistance and opens a channel for understanding and acceptance. My willingness unleashed psychic energy that, at times, was like a tidal wave. When I could experience my psychic energy with calmness, I was fascinated by it. Most of the time I felt overwhelmed by it and, in truth, I feared it.

As I talked to my inner psychic, or rather, she talked to me, I understood how my attempts to control her allowed her to control me. I cried, and told her that I was afraid of her. I heard the voices of others from my childhood saying, "You know too much" and "You're too smart for your own good". My mother was psychic and afraid of her own powers. She once said to me "Knowing too much can hurt us." As a child I instinctively knew I wanted to avoid being hurt and decided not to "know too much."

Once I acknowledged this inner self, the Psychic, I knew there was no turning back. Her power was intense and I could no longer disown or deny her. My next step was to be willing to face my fears about her. Eventually I faced my fear of aloneness and separation from others.

Identifying and getting to know your inner selves is a process that leads to greater and greater self-understanding and self-acceptance. And it is an ongoing process. It takes time and a good deal of gentle reassuring to reestablish trust with your inner selves; but your time is rewarded by a growing sense of integrity and wholeness.

Each of us is a unique and complete individual. Each of our inner selves is a worthy part of us. Self-esteem comes from owning, accepting, and valuing all of our inner selves. By giving gentle and loving attention to all of our inner selves, we heal by restoring our natural balance.

Early Childhood Exploration

Early childhood exploration, often linked with

Inner Child work and Identification of Inner Selves, is very powerful healing medicine. As innocent children we are very impressionable. We take to heart the direct and hidden messages we receive from our surroundings. Because of our innocence we are indiscriminate. We are like little sponges who soak up the words and feelings of those around us, often adding our own childish interpretations. We register and record our collection of messages and, over time, we treat the record of messages as our own. It is important, at some point in life, to stop, play the recording, and erase most of the messages in the collection.

We have personal power, the abilities of conscious awareness and choice. We were programmed before we could grow into our personal power. We can go back and erase the messages that do not serve our right and good purpose.

Early childhood work is simple but not easy. It is a process like most other healing approaches that, once begun, becomes an ongoing part of your life, a part of your healing diet. Once you commit to the process, you can accomplish a good deal in a short time. But, our early childhood messages are stored on onion-like records. We need to continually peel away the layers.

The process takes guts. On a deep level, you are ultimately dealing with the exposure of all your worst fears. Your commitment in Early Childhood exploration is a commitment to come face-to-face with your dark side, your shadow side. In the beginning, you may find it helpful to get support from others. Therapists and other professionals can show you the ropes and provide training in technique and process. They can provide a safe and comfortable space for you to begin. It is important to realize, though, that ultimately, early childhood work is a job you do alone. No one can do it for you. It is yours and yours alone.

The reason for this is simple. The biggest fear for each of us is the fear of being alone. It is the root of all other fears. Sooner or later, this is the one you have to tackle. It is definitely a solo job. That is precisely what it is all about. No one else can get you through this one. Your own "dark night of the soul" is for you and you alone. Your willingness to face the big fear and push through your deepest darkness is your opportunity for rebirth and recreation.

Facing the ultimate fear, fear of aloneness, is the reason many people avoid beginning early childhood exploration and the reason others cut the process short. But, like most things, practice makes the process easier. Taken one bite at a time, one small fear by one small fear, the road can take you gently to the big one.

My journey back to early childhood started with the jolting realization that I had spent much of my life, Part I, operating out of a fear of abandonment. It was a jolting realization because I really thought I did not have any "issues" around abandonment. That my parents separated when I was eight years old and my father literally disappeared from my life, never seemed to be a problem for me. I did such a good job of burying this experience that it took forty more years for the impact to be felt. After my father disappeared when I was eight, I spent the next forty years creating a world of people who would die, disappear, or were incapable of being there for me. That, of course, led to the big one, the fear of being alone, and I got to have my dark night of the soul.

As part of my early childhood healing work I decided I needed to know whether my father was dead or alive. My mother had died a year and a half earlier. I had reached a very comfortable place with my mother and had a wonderful sense of completion with her life. In the spirit of handling unfinished business, I wanted to know the status of my father. I contacted an elderly brother and discovered my father was alive, had been institutionalized for years, and did not recognize anyone. This was not what I realized I wanted to hear. I wanted to hear that he was dead. If he had already died, I could do my own deep healing work and come to closure. It took me a little while to realize that I could still do it and I did.

In the middle of writing this section on healing, I got a call saying my father had just died. His death brought up grief for all the recent losses in my life, but little of it had to do with my father. I had already reached a place of closure with him. I now had to deal with how I had projected my father's emotional abuse, and then abandonment, into my adult life.

Personal Peak Experience Identification

Personal Peak Experience Identification is the light twin of the Early Childhood work, which, admittedly, can be heavy. In identifying your Personal Peak Experiences, you get to revisit the situations and events that made you feel happy, successful, alive, and, well, really you. On the face of it, this sounds like a fairly simple process. The only problem is, some people have buried these experiences deep in the subconscious and it is difficult to recall them. And some people, in recalling peak experiences, discover that they were only peak experiences in the eyes of other people, experiences that got outward approval from others with little or no self-satisfaction.

Identifying Personal Peak Experiences can take some time, effort, and sorting out. But, again, the time is well worth it, especially if you are attempting to put together a new game plan for yourself. Take the time to go back in time. What were the experiences and situations where you felt really good about yourself, all connected, and flowing? What personal accomplishments gave you great self-satisfaction? If you have always been an overachiever, you may have a long list of successes. Sift through the successes. Go beyond the experiences that brought outside approval and recognition only. Find those experiences that brought self-satisfaction and a sense of wholeness and integrity. They may be the same experiences. They may not.

You have the ability to reexperience your most satisfying events and moments and, in reexperiencing, you regenerate your current sense of personal power. Don't believe it when others tell you, "You can't go back". You can, if only in memory. Yet the reexperiencing of vivid memories along with positive emotions is one of the most effective healing approaches. You actually get to recreate and reignite your own positive energy.

Past Life Exploration

Past life exploration, regression, can be helpful in healing. I believe that the soul, or spirit energy, continues from one incarnation to the next. I do not believe the popular notion that the soul progresses from one lifetime to the next, ever seeking perfection. This is the sin and punishment notion where, lifetime through lifetime, we are ever struggling, trying to get it right and paying for past lifetime mistakes. This is a false definition of karma.

The soul moves from one lifetime, one physical energy experience, to the next, because it must. The essence of Universal Energy is movement and change. The energy moves through a cycle of life, death, and life again changing from spiritual to physical and spiritual energy again.

The choice of the spirit is not progression to perfection from one lifetime to another. The soul, in choosing a birth moment, selects for variety. In other words, you choose a lifetime for the unique experience it has to offer. Each lifetime holds the potential of a different game to play, a new lifetime adventure. *Each lifetime is complete and perfect in itself.*

We need carry no baggage from lifetime to lifetime. Yet, we often do. We often, unknowingly and subconsciously, carry over experiences, especially negative feelings and emotions from past lifetimes. Things have a tendency to stick to us. The value of past life exploration is in discovering the baggage we have inappropriately brought into this life experience. Going back to a previous lifetime may give you insight into some attitude or behavior you are holding in this life-time. You may then examine whether the old attitude or behavior is relevant to this lifetime or merely a carryover, excess baggage. In many cases, your deci-sion will be to jettison the useless cargo. There may also be aspects of past lives that you will choose to keep because they serve a useful purpose to you in this life experience.

Again, each of your soul's life experiences is com-plete and perfect in itself. From your past life experi-ences, choose what serves your purpose on this life path and dump the excess baggage.

This goes for people, too. You may discover that some of the people in your life are carryovers from past life experiences. People tend to stick also. And, while it is true that everyone in your life is there for a reason, it may be that some folks are "stickers" from past lives. It may be for you to discover who is a hold-over and who is a positive player in your current life adventure. Another possibility is that you may be hold-ing onto agreements made with certain people in past lives. For instance, you may discover, through regres-sion, that you made a previous agreement to take care of someone and you discover that you are operating out of that old agreement in this lifetime. Remember, each lifetime is whole and complete in itself.

Your purpose in each lifetime is to live out that life as fully and constructively as possible. The end goal is to arrive at balance, the state of grace. It is up to you to choose whether to carryover or "renew" past agree-ments with others in this lifetime. *The completion of each lifetime cancels all debts.*

Play

In outlining healing approaches, the last one is the best one. Play. Goof off. Have some leisure time. Take a break. Play some more. We all know how to play. Many of us don't play. We don't play because we were taught as young children that we need permission to play. Some of us play anyway, then feel guilty for playing and turn the guilt inward. Some of us hide our play or disguise it as something serious or socially acceptable until our play gets twisted and we start to believe our play is not play. We do all sorts of things with play; but play is a basic and healthy need. We need to be silly, light, and childlike at times. We need to get away from our adult concerns. We need room to daydream.

Play reconnects us with our original child selves and our innocence. It is not only okay to play, it is necessary. When you play you generate light energy which brings your spirit, mind, emotions, and body into balance. Play. Play openly and play with gusto.

Embrace change. Life is change. As you begin to heal, change in your life begins to accelerate. One of the kindest and most loving things you can do for yourself during your conscious healing is to *detach from outcomes*. We make plans, take actions, and expect certain results and outcomes.

Most of us have tried to control results and have been disappointed when things did not turn out exactly as we planned. In conscious healing, we can be wiser. We can trust in our Godpower and accept the changes without expectations. We can flow with the unfolding of our life pattern. It is a perfect, complete pattern that will sustain and support us.

Part III

Transformation

Introduction _____

Major life changes are hell. Loss and separation, any-time in life, but especially during mid-life, is usually devastating. This is particularly true when there are multiple losses that impact many different areas of life. When the slate is wiped clean, it is not always possible to see any opportunity.

It is hard to hear, let alone take seriously, the advice of others. "Just give it time and things will get better." "Life goes on," and, my personal favorite, "The sun will come up tomorrow." Others' words have a hollow sound. You are sure they are just mouthing words of consolation, words they read in a book somewhere. You begin to feel like the butt of every cosmic joke. Your hopelessness is beyond Hallmark's remedy.

Our culture's attitudes about major life changes are that they are sad, inevitable, parts of life that must be grimly endured. Most of the help and resources available center around coping. The many books titled "How-To-Deal With...", "How-To-Manage Your...", and "How-To-Live-With..." reflect the common notion that major life transitions are simply natural breaks in the pattern of your life. Time and coping will eventually enable you to move on and continue along your path. Most counseling programs and support groups are developed and conducted by well-intentioned and caring people who are sincere in their efforts to help you get through your difficult time.

An outstanding exception to the many resources that offer little more than coping techniques is the Recovery Movement with its emphasis on restoring wholeness to lives ripped apart by loss, separation, and change. Twelve Step Programs offer the opportunity to restore yourself to the wholeness of your early childhood self. All of the Twelve-Step Programs of the Recovery Movement require direct involvement in your own restoration. In Recovery Programs you learn to accept that you and your Higher Power, the term for the Universal Energy of Love or God, are co-creators of your life. You learn that the only way to recover your childlike wholeness is by taking personal responsibility for your past, present, and future.

The Twelve Steps Programs, some of which include Alcoholics Anonymous, Adult Children of Alcoholics, Al-Anon, Narcotics Anonymous, Overeaters Anonymous, and Co-Dependents Anonymous, offer support groups where participants come together in safe space to share their experiences and support each other. Recovery programs are important resources for personal healing during major life transitions.

Personal transformation is the approach that takes you the next step, the full step. It is only through your wholehearted commitment to personal healing then transformation, that you are able to move into the full expression of yourself and your uniqueness in relation to all others. The path of personal transformation moves you from the level of survivor to thriver. The path of full self-expression leads past coping as your destination toward fully living and celebrating your life. *Personal transformation involves learning to live in love, the highest form of self-expression.*

Steps to Living In Love _____

Practically everything in our culture and society, and in our upbringing and traditions, represents an obstacle to living in love. The idea that it is only by loving others that we can truly love ourselves permeates our lives. At every step of the way, we hear the message that we can only experience love through the reflection of others.

As women, we learned early that the greatest gift is to give of ourselves. Give it away. Give in. Give it up. At the same time, we were bombarded by a barrage of messages that told us we had to look outside ourselves for true happiness and well-being. We learned that we should focus on others' well-being and, by concentrating our focus outside ourselves, others' love would fill us up.

But here is the catch. You cannot get love. You must be love. You cannot attract what you do not first project. You cannot have what you are not already. Love, in its purest form, is the ultimate energy. It is the most powerful of life forces. It is that which connects each to the other and all to the one. In order to attract love, we must radiate love. In order to radiate love, it must come from within each one of us individually. In order to catch the reflection of the love of others, we must first be filled to overflowing with love for ourselves.

There can be no question but that to love ourselves is to be totally, wonderfully selfish. In being totally, wonderfully selfish, truly selfish, we can then radiate our own magnificence and completeness. The expression of the pure joy of our own self-acceptance, self-respect, and self-loving overflows. The pure energy of our love for ourselves is the energy that radiates outward and reflects back to us the love of others. *There is only one way to live in love. You must love yourself with all your heart. You must love yourself completely and unconditionally.* Never judge. Never criticize. Talk to yourself in only the most gentle and caring way. How you treat yourself will radiate outward and be reflected back from others and, in fact, the whole universe.

If love does not come from outside of you, if love does not first come from others, where does it come from? Remember that love, as all things, is energy. Everything in the universe is energy. Material things are energy in physical form — our bodies, houses, personal items, pets, plant life, etc. And money. Money is energy in physical form. Just about everything we touch is energy in physical form. Even though all this energy in physical form is vast and takes up much of what we perceive as real, the physical dimension is but an aspect of Universal Energy. Spiritual energy is also an aspect of what we "touch" as physical, material energy plus ALL things we cannot "touch". All forces in the universe are spiritual energy. All thoughts, ideas, and feelings are spiritual energy. All spiritual energy is part of Universal Energy which is limitless and can be accessed by each of us.

We are all part of the One Universal Energy. We are all connected. No one is separate or operates alone. It cannot be that way. Through individual awareness, which is energy, we are all connected to each other with the One Universal Energy.

The purest form of Universal Energy is spiritual energy experienced and expressed as love. Love is the highest vibration of light. It is the purest transforming energy. Open yourself to receive as much light as possible. Remember that Universal Energy is limitless. Fill yourself with love. Fill yourself to overflowing and know that the overflow is what connects you to others. You are part of the One Universal Energy. You are unique. You are perfect. You are complete when you tap into and fill yourself to overflowing with the Universal light energy of love. You are *enlightened.*

If you plug into the giant Universal Energy love generator every day, you can experience enlightenment every day. Make a commitment to live in the light of love.

At first, this takes some conscious effort and practice. It is important to identify experiences that help you trigger tapping into love, the light energy. I have always been a "nature freak", although there were years in my life where I lost track of this and got out of touch. It is now vitally important for me to be out of doors some of the time.

I take great pleasure in gardening and, even through the last four difficult years, gardening has been my "therapy". It is the ease and flow of nature, the sense of natural balance, that fills me with peace. I open myself to receiving this love energy. I have come to appreciate the lightness and easiness that operates in nature. I have learned to experience this in my own garden. I spend less time and effort now. I tend and encourage my herbs and perennials and spend the rest of my time appreciating my garden.

I love the water, especially the ocean, and am always filled with a sense of wonder at how plentiful the love energy is there. I love woods and the night sky. Experiencing the outdoors in all its many aspects is my way of tapping into the Universal Energy of Love.

Surely, this is not the only way. In fact, it is not the only way I practice tapping into enlightenment. There are many ways. Once you sense that there is One energy and each of us is part of that One Energy, you can begin to see it in many different ways. To begin to consciously tap into that energy, find a way that works for you and keep at it. Fill yourself with Universal Love. Then love yourself to overflowing. Your great outpouring of love merges with others' outpouring of love.

Here is my top ten list of steps to living in love. The list is, by no means, definitive. The steps on the list are not incremental. The only priority is the first step. The rest are all equally important and represent a well-balanced approach to getting there. You can add your own steps. I expect, as time and my life goes on, I may add new dimensions to some of these steps also. There is one step that I do not ever expect to change in any way. It is the first step and it is the foundation step of living in love:

1. *Love Yourself and Who You Are.* Completely, totally, and unconditionally.

2. *Rediscover Your Dreams and Follow Them.*

What are your dreams? Do you know anymore? Many of us go through life burying our dreams. We cover them over with others' notions of what is real, what is practical, and how things can and cannot be done. We sometimes give our dreams away or give the power for making our dreams come true to others. We begin to believe that life is about playing by the rules until many of us reach a point where all we have to show for it is the certain knowledge that we played by the rules. Then we begin to question the game, and that's a good starting point.

A good way to begin to rediscover your dreams is by understanding your astrological birthchart. It is all there — your original self with all your dreams and visions, your unique talents, abilities, and potential. Another good way to rediscover and reconstruct your dreams is through early childhood and inner selves exploration. These approaches can help you identify your earliest yearnings, urges, and desires. What did you imagine as a child? What were your daydreams about?

When you identify your dreams, you tap into your original self. When you commit to following your dreams, which are the natural expression of your creativity, you unleash a powerful energy flow that attracts cooperation from everything outside you. Your dreams are extremely strong energy. Once you begin to act on them, your personal power begins to resonate with the rest of the universe. In following your dreams, identifying what is right and natural for you, you become the creator of your own life, your own game, in harmony with God's plan for you. You put your piece of the great energy circuit into balance and harmony.

No dream is too large or too small. It is not necessary to have a huge dream, and it is okay to follow a new and different dream from time to time. Sometimes the joy of following your dream is the creation and playing of your own game. When that is done, its time to play a new game. Most of us had lots of dreams. Rediscover some of them. As you begin to identify some of your dreams, you will soon begin to remember more.

Generally, there are two things that stop us from following our dreams. The first is considered by most of us to be a good thing -our values and ideals. The second is considered to be the bad thing — our fears.

Most of us have been brought up to believe that our values are a constant in our lives and that they are sacred. Our values shape our attitudes about everything — work, family, relationships, finances, friendship, health, play, etc. If you are going to rediscover and follow your dreams, you have to begin to question every single value and ideal you have held sacred. *The only certainty in the universe is motion and change.* You will most likely discover that you are clinging to some values and ideals that no longer work for you. You may also discover that certain values and ideals never did work for you. You may also discover that you have been living out of values that were never really yours — most often the values passed along family lines, sometimes back through several generations.

In my experience, this was an extremely difficult and painful process, especially when I came to the realization that almost every one of my values and ideals came into question. I had to reexamine my notions that involved forever — especially forever friendships and relationships. I had to reexamine the value of loyalty. I had to reexamine the value of family. At the end of my life, Part 1, in order to create and follow the next life path, I had to come face-to-face with the need to let go of almost everything I had previously been guided by. In the process of letting go of the worn-out values, I felt a tremendous sense of loss and grief, yet I knew, on a very deep level, that the universe was giving me an important opportunity to change and move more freely with my new life direction. I let go and let go and let go, and trusted that the flow of the new current would carry me.

The most important thing I learned from this experience is the importance of constantly questioning your values and ideals. What worked for you before may not serve you any longer. We need to be aware of our values and the need for change. We need to be cautious about accepting others' values. A good thing is only a good thing if it supports your unique self expression and life direction.

The other thing that stops us from following our dreams is our fears. There are two ways to approach handling your fears. You can go at them one by one in a piecemeal fashion and look at your fear of success, fear of failure, fear of not having enough, fear of not being enough, fear of not being accepted, fear of not being approved, fear of being weak, fear of being strong, etc. All of these are legitimate human fears and, if one of these is a particular issue for you, by all means, start there.

My suggestion to the courageous, or, as was my case, desperate, is to go right to the big one — the fear of aloneness. This is the ultimate human fear. All other psychological fears stem from the fear of aloneness.

Many of us have built our lives around aloneness prevention. The fear of being alone is reflected everywhere in our culture. There is nothing worse than being old and alone, or young and alone, or sick and alone, or happy and alone. Have you ever gone to a restaurant by yourself and been greeted with, "Just one?" In a society where Barbara Streisand sings, "People who need people are the luckiest people in the world," we have all been trained from early childhood to feel sad for people who are alone. Our cultural fear of aloneness, it seems, is a reflection of an even more deep seated fear — *the fear of individualism and the power of one.*

Try as we may to prevent ever being alone, our every effort is ultimately frustrated. Whether surrounded by friends and family members or by oneself in a hospital room, WE ALL DIE ALONE. No one can make the crossing with us. We do it alone.

It seems impossible to me to face the fear of aloneness without having been healed spiritually. Our very interconnectedness to each other and to all energy forms, both physical and spiritual, makes aloneness an impossibility. When all of nature and the cosmos vibrate to the same universal music, how can we possibly experience ourselves as separate from that? It is the very oneness of each individual in full expression that brings all of the Universal Energy into harmony. *To celebrate your aloneness, your oneness, is to celebrate your unconditional love for everything in the universe.*

3. *Recognize Your Conditioning and RECONDITION Yourself.*

There are those who choose a conscious path of detaching from their egos and identities in pursuit of personal transcendence. There are others whose life paths lead them through a maze of experiences that results in loss of ego and identity. In either case, for many of us, there comes a time in our lives when we must rediscover our lost or buried selves. My life path experiences led to my need to reach back to an earlier self that had been lost to me. Over recent years I had given away most of myself and my identity.

When I came face-to-face with the emptiness reflected in my life, the void I had created soon was filled with a longing for my old self. This internal longing took me back to childhood and a rediscovery of my early adulthood. Through intensive work with reawakening my inner child, I discovered issues that I thought were not issues in my life. In experiencing my own identity death, I "accidentally" unburied issues that I thought I had long ago resolved.

The process was frightening because it brought a sense of disorientation. How could I have become so

out of touch with myself? How could I have gone unconscious to some of the very issues that had run my
life for most of my adult life? The more fear I felt in
exposing the bones buried in my subconscious, the
more acutely aware I became of the opportunity I had
to expose and purge old concepts and ideas. The more
committed I became to the process, the more easily
the old bones rose to the surface.

Once I accepted a kind of opening of the flood-
gates to my unconscious and my past, a tidal wave of
old notions, thoughts, ideas, and messages rushed to
the surface. My physical reaction was immediate and
powerful. My body started to shed toxins that had been
poisoning me for a long time. As I reexperienced hearing the voices and messages of early childhood, I also
saw quite clearly how I had let some of those messages
run my adult life.

At first, I felt a sense of amazement that buried
thoughts and messages could really affect the course
of my life. Yet, at the same time, I understood that, for
each of us, how we live out our childhood patterns is
inherent in each of our unique destinies. It is the wheel
of life ever moving toward completion. It is the pattern reflected in the birthchart. For some of us, part
of our pattern is to completely lose ourselves so we can
experience all the sensation attendant with rediscovering and recreating ourselves.

The process of rediscovery, especially with respect
to early childhood work, involves uncovering and ex-
amining the notions and messages that have run our
personal show to date. As an astrologer, I highly recommend the birthchart as a way of understanding your-

self. If you take the time to learn some astrology, you will definitely benefit by the process. You can also choose to work with a professional in interpreting the language of symbols in your chart. In either case, you will undoubtedly find that this is a highly effective and timesaving method for doing personal rediscovery work.

There are other ways, of course. Once you realize you have to do some early child and inner child work and make a commitment to it, you will open a channel to discovering the right approach that works for you.

Each of us has to find our own unique way of opening growth and healing channels. Once we sense our direction, listen to ourselves and learn to trust that that is how the channel opens for us, we have to trust and surrender ourselves to it completely.

Throughout my life, almost as soon as I identify a need for outside information or support, a book almost magically appears in my hands. As I look back at the turning points in my life, each experience has been supported by a special book that led me on the next step of my path. For me and my birth pattern, the vibration of the planet Mercury in its many forms of communication, especially books and information, has been the operative channel.

I have had the perfect book jump into my hands so many times in my life, that, I have come to trust that these events are totally natural for me. I have also come to trust my innate ability to make connections with the right people at the right time. Almost as soon as I identify a certain connection I need to make, the person to make the connection appears.

I knew that part of the process of recreating myself and moving toward wholeness was reacquainting myself with my body. Over the course of recent years, I had become somewhat out of touch with my physical self. Intellectually, I knew that by listening to my body, I could get major clues to the big picture of my life. But the events and circumstances in my life became so overwhelming that the messages from my body seemed only to reinforce how out of control it all was. Most of the time my body only reflected back pain.

As I experienced my own dying and began to sense a need to rediscover and recreate myself, my body seemed to lead the way. I realized that my physical sensations had been about ten steps ahead of me. All I had to do was listen to what my body was telling me and I would be moved to the next step. There was incredible comfort and relief in realizing my own body had the potential to guide me toward recovering the rest of myself.

I realized that one of the early and important aspects of my rediscovery and healing was the physical aspect. I wanted to explore the physical-emotional healing connection through message therapy. Near the official end of my relationship breakup, I needed to get away. My partner had chosen to move herself and her business out of the house we shared for the last fourteen of our twenty-four years. She needed the space to conduct her move and I needed to be on another planet. At the suggestion of one friend, I reconnected with other friends who had just retired to the sunny south. As I began my drive to Florida from Upstate New York, I vowed to find a message therapist and begin some physical healing. I never even got a chance to mention this because, no sooner did I arrive, when my friends excitedly told me about the new people I would get a chance to meet. One just happened to be a message therapist! Needless to say, I had just experienced another wonderful and seemingly effortless connection.

The more fascinated I have become with this seemingly miraculous happening, the more open I have become, and the more quickly and easily it seems to happen. Put yourself in the space of healing. Get still and listen carefully to yourself. What is your body, your mind, your heart, telling you. What do you need? How can you give it to yourself? Project your needs outward. Your thoughts are energy. The energy radiates and attracts what you project.

Take some time to observe what you attract with ease. This is a good starting place. For me, it has always been books and information. Over my lifetime, I have come to depend on this. It is my channel of ease. We all have *channels of ease*, those areas of our lives where we have always had an easy time. Maybe it is attracting just the person you need for a specific lesson you need to learn. Maybe it is being in what turns out to be the right place. Maybe it is having just the right utensil or tool for the job. Maybe it is knowing how to create just the right utensil or tool for the job.

Most of us tend to take what we do with ease for granted. We labor under the assumption that, if it is easy, it is not worth much. We often feel, if it is easy, we do not deserve it or value it. Quite the contrary. Identifying and operating through our channels of ease is the most personally rewarding thing we can do.

Recognize your conditioning, then set out to recondition yourself. Do not work at it. Do it with ease. Take it easy and be easy on yourself. Let your healing be gentle and flowing. Talk kindly to yourself. Build your rediscovery of yourself on a foundation of easiness and your natural flow and rhythm.

4. *Seek Out and Surround Yourself With Positive People.*

The best way to begin to live in love is to seek out others who are living in the light. Positive people appreciate and support other positive people. Like attracts like. When you are talking about transforming your life into a love-generating experience, it is vital that you seek out good, strong support. Do not look for gurus. There aren't any. If you make someone a guru you give your own personal power away. You need people who will support you becoming you. The good news is that it is relatively easy to find these people. These are the people who are involved in groups and programs that support their own self-discovery and transformation. My personal recommendations for linking up with positive support people are Unity Church and the Church of Religious Science, most Twelve-Step programs and their support groups, and most nontraditional healers and practitioners. Almost any New Age group has the potential for meeting others seeking the light.

However, remember, no gurus. Any group or individual who espouses their way as the only way is not, in the end, going to support your unique growth and development. In all cases, use your discretion. Trust yourself. If someone does not feel positive to you, they are not positive for you.

The other side of this step is sometimes more difficult and even more necessary. You have to move away from negative people. Negative people can destroy you, especially in your beginning stages of transformation. Negative people have little love and respect for themselves and infect everyone around them. These are the needy people whose reaction to outside help is to become ever more needy. These are the people that sap your energy as they try to drag you down with them. It is important to realize that these people cannot be helped until they decide to help themselves. They cannot be loved until they love themselves. Be tolerant and understanding of these people; but do not let them block your path.

5. *Express Your Sense of Humor.*

While play is critical to healing, expressing your sense of humor is important to transformation. We all have a sense of humor. If you think you don't have a sense of humor, change your mind. You have one. Maybe you lost it, lots of us did; but decide, right now, to find it again. You cannot transform yourself without it.

Expressing your sense of humor ignites and generates your light energy. Transformation hinges on your ability to look on the light side, take things lightly, and lighten up. Laughter loosens and jolts the light energy right out of you and multiplies the light energy around you. Laughter also gets you double points. It works for your healing and it works for your transformation.

You are not crazy if your tears at one moment are followed by laughter at the next moment. You are healthy. In fact, your ability to lighten up after a good cry is a sign that you are on the right track to experiencing your own wholeness.

Look for at least two good laughs a day. A good laugh is one that tickles your own sense of the ridiculous or the absurd. It can be an especially good laugh when you see your own part in the ridiculous or absurd. This is the ability to laugh at yourself, especially when you catch yourself taking things too seriously.

One of my best memories of transformative laughter at a time when I was really looking for it came from a support group in which I participated. When it was her time to share what was on her mind, one of our members began to rapidly rattle off a litany of "do gooder" behaviors she was just plain tired of but seemed unable to stop. Her delivery was elegant in its simplicity. Before she could finish a great wave of laughter broke out in the room. She had created a wonderful, synchronous moment where each of us in the room personally identified with her. We laughed at ourselves, with each other, and at the ridiculousness of it all. The laughter was the highlight of that day's meeting and, interestingly enough, seemed to move the whole group into a lighter space in future meetings.

Recreating and reinventing yourself, transformation, can sometimes seem like serious business. Remember that the whole point of transformation is to turn yourself into a light energy generator. If you get into effort and struggle, as we are prone to do from time to time, back off, lighten up, and get your balance. Laughter lightens the load.

6. *Use the Thought/Feeling Connection to Your Best Advantage.*

Your thoughts reflect your feelings and your feelings reflect your thoughts. Feelings and thoughts are interconnected, so much so, that many philosophies collapse the two into one and express the whole person as body, mind, and spirit. There is an assumption that emotions are included in the mind aspect and the implication that the mind and emotions operate as one. By referring to both as mind, there is the further implication that mind takes precedent over emotions. We know how that has played out in our culture. The value of human emotion has all but disappeared.

Mind and emotion are two separate and equal aspects. Mind is the air element. Emotion is the water element. Mind is thoughts. Emotion is feelings. The whole person is spirit, body, mind, and emotion; fire, earth, air, and water.

Mind, your air element, is thoughts, ideas, and attitudes. Together, they make up your perceptions — what you believe to be real. We, therefore, each create our own reality with our thoughts, ideas, and attitudes which are our unique perceptions. No one else can think your thoughts, get your ideas, or have your attitudes. Your perceptions are uniquely yours. The reality you create is your own.

Emotion, the water element, is your feelings. Your

feelings of joy, gratitude, contentment, bliss, anger, sadness, grief, frustration, and happiness, together, operate as a barometer measuring your satisfaction in relation to the reality you have created. Your feelings are your feelings. No one else can feel your feelings. They are uniquely yours. They are very important and very real.

Emotion is your personal radar system,. As your radar system, your emotion detects and provides feedback on the status of your reality. Emotion reflects the status of your inner reality in relation to outside reality. If you do not feel your feelings, you lose your barometer and get "out of touch" with the reality you have created. When you acknowledge your feelings you fully tune in to your radar system.

The thing that prevents many of us from keeping our radar systems fully engaged and feeling our feelings is fear. Emotional and mental, or psychological, pain, as well as physical pain, and our fear of the unknown, often block us from coming face-to-face with our individually created realities. We fear feeling because we fear the content of what might be reflected back to us.

All of this fear stems from the too commonly held notion that we are powerless over our thoughts and feelings. Your thoughts are your thoughts. Your feelings are your feelings. You cannot help it, it is just the way you are. Right? While it is vitally important to respect your own thoughts and your own feelings, that is self-acceptance, you also have total ownership and control over your reality. If you do not like your reality, if some part of it does not feel good to you, CHANGE IT.

You have full and complete power to change your reality at any time you choose. This idea has been around for a long time but, from my experience, the popular advice for how to change reality is backwards. The cultural message is too often directed at emotion, probably due to the low value we place on this aspect. There is both open and hidden pressure to change how we feel and we have all become infected with it. Cheer up. Be happy. Don't be sad. Don't feel that way about it. Smile.

The power to change your reality is in not changing your feelings but feeling your feelings so you can change your thoughts. Your thoughts, ideas, and attitudes — your perception — is your reality. If your feelings reflect something you do not like, something that does not feel good to you, or something that does not work for you, then you can change your thoughts, change your ideas, and change your attitudes to get a different perspective and a changed reality. Changing your feelings does not change your perceptions, it only cuts you off from your own radar. Accepting the assistance from your feelings to change your thoughts is the only way to take full advantage of the partnership. In some cases, when you change your thinking, your feelings will change also, but, in my experience, it doesn't happen the other way around.

In changing your reality you are actually changing your response pattern to the circumstances of your life. Your circumstances are your circumstances. They are the happenings imbedded in your life pattern. Your reality is a combination of your happenings and your response to the happenings. You cannot always change your circumstances, but you can influence many of them. You can always change your perceptions.

Realistically, this is a process that may take some time. If you are at all compulsive in your thinking and feeling behaviors, it may take some real effort as well. Life changes and transitions tend to emphasize our feelings of powerlessness and being out-of-control. It is easy to slip into compulsive negative thinking. From my own experience and from working with many compulsive thinking and feeling clients, if you are compulsive you are compulsive. It is possible, however, to change the quality of your compulsiveness. Recognize that your negative compulsive thinking is an unhealthy habit and begin to shift to positive compulsive thinking. It takes some time and self-acceptance to break a bad habit. Substituting positive for negative thoughts is a good place to start.

There is one more important piece to changing your reality and that is the action step. Sometimes changing your perception does not get you a better reading on your emotional barometer. Sometimes a lousy job is a lousy job and, no matter how you change your thoughts about it, you still feel unappreciated and undervalued. Change your perceptions first, then check with your feelings. If you still get the same feelings after you have changed your perceptions, you may need to change your perceptions again or, more likely, you need to take some action. Look for a new job. Changing your perceptions only will keep you stuck "living in your head." The action step is important and you have to pick and choose. More on this in the Temperance and timing step.

7. *Keep Moving Forward.*

Moving forward is moving toward and into the light, the lightness of positive Universal Energy. Each day, dedicate yourself to filling yourself to overflowing with light energy. In the day, bask in the sunshine. At night, bask in moonglow. Revel in the energy of the sun and moon and know that, through your interconnectedness, you are the sun and moon.

Your journey of transformation is a forward movement, an alignment with Universal motion and change. Some healing steps require you to look back. If you are committed to transformation as well as healing, then realize that the "looking back" involved in deep inner healing serves you because it is used for your ultimate moving forward. Keep your "looking back" contained in your healing work. Other than those times when you are involved in specific healing work, keep moving forward. Outside of the space of your conscious healing work, *don't look back.* This is extremely important. As the co-creator of your new life, the co-source and co-director of your personal power, you define and direct the energy. Keep the energy you define and work with in your healing space separate from the light-only energy of the rest of your space, your transformation space.

In the beginning of your reinventing yourself, you will probably need to give a good deal of your personal space to healing and perhaps only a little space to transformation. As the process goes on and you are becoming healed, you can easily begin to shift toward more and more transformation space. The key, of course, is balance. Do not allow yourself to get stuck in your head by thinking you "should" do this or that for your healing. Pay attention to yourself. Listen to your feelings, mind, body, and spirit. Begin to give as much space to transformation and moving ahead as soon as you possibly can.

Allow yourself time for your continuous healing work because it is an ongoing process. At the same time, begin to create greater and greater personal space for transformation. Continue the shift until all of your space outside of your defined healing work is dedicated to your transformation, your moving ahead into the light.

I have found a very simple approach to moving ahead. It involves asking yourself three simple questions:

1. "Does this serve my highest purpose?"
2. "Does this contribute to my overall balance and sense of well-being?"
3. "Does it feel good?"

If you are doing something and get a "no" to any of your three questions, STOP DOING IT. If you are deciding whether to do something and get a "no" to any of your three questions, DON'T DO IT. If you are thinking something, run your three questions by your thoughts. If you get a "no" about something you are thinking, STOP THINKING IT.

Practice the three question approach for awhile. Use it as a test for everything in your life. In transformation you are recreating and reinventing your life. You get to throw out everything that does not support your best forward movement.

When the three question approach has become

automatic for you, you can begin to work with the question that synthesizes and summarizes the first three: "Does this support my moving forward into the light?"

Transformation involves conscious awareness and choice. It involves constantly choosing what supports your highest and best purpose. It involves fearlessly saying no to that which diminishes your highest and best purpose.

Whether or not you have clearly identified your dreams and personal life purpose, we all have one, ultimate, unifying purpose. The ultimate purpose for each of us is to love. Live, love, light, breath, and spirit all come from the same source meaning — the purest expression of the energy of being. They also grow from the same root — the heart.

8. *Live SIMPLY, HARMLESSLY, and GRACIOUSLY.*

Living simply is possible when you understand that there is Limitless Abundance in our universe. There is always enough and you need only take what you need now. Your needs tomorrow will be supplied.

Complication blocks the flow of light energy. Many of us let our lives become too complicated. Too much depends on too much else. Too many things pile up in layers of too many things. We have tangled webs of relationships and friendships. We have twisted lines of responsibilities and agreements. We have stockpiles of toys and "stuff." We realize all we have in our lives is distraction and clutter and, suddenly, its all too much.

To live simply is to live in the flow of your life

without unnecessary distraction and clutter. Living simply means eliminating complication. It means identifying what supports your self-expression. It means focusing on what sustains your uniqueness and recognizing that as your life unfolds your needs change. Eliminate what no longer supports who you are. Get rid of the clutter, the excess baggage. There is limitless abundance in the universe. You are entitled to have whatever you need. If you do not need it now, let it go. Simplify your life and open the channels to receive light energy. Celebrate the wonder of life's simple gifts. These are the real treasures.

The second part of this step is to make a commitment to live harmlessly. This concept involves increasing your awareness and then living out of your conscious intentions. Most of us try not to hurt others, but we have lived with that intention for so long, since we were children, that it has been a long time since we examined what that involves. To make a commitment to live harmlessly means to continuously examine and reexamine how our attitudes and actions affect others. We are all connected and are part of the One Universal Energy. Everything in the physical world from the whole of Mother Earth to the smallest of wildlife is wondrously interrelated. Because of your marvelous connection to everyone and everything else, what you do to yourself has an effect on everything else. When your attitudes and actions toward yourself are healthy and gentle, your outward expression reflects your self-respect. Living harmlessly means right thinking and taking care of yourself in positive ways that support who you are.

When you come from this approach and take assertive and personal responsibility for yourself, you create an environment that supports, not harms, yourself, others, and the physical world around you.

The third part of this step is to commit to living graciously. To live graciously is to live with zest and elan. It is to live lightly and easily. Gracious living is the partner to simple living. Simplicity provides clarity and a sense of personal priority. Graciousness adds class and the aesthetic touch.

Taken together, simplicity and graciousness allow you to focus on and appreciate that which supports your completeness and full self-expression so you may experience your life as a work of art.

9. *Cultivate Temperance and Timing*

Temperance and timing, together, equal the flow of your life. Temperance is your state of perfect balance. It is the right expression of your fire, earth, air, and water qualities as is natural for you. You reach a state of temperance when you recognize that the expression of your energy, a unique expression of the One Universal Energy, is controlled by your will. The purpose of your will is to express and experience all things in moderation, all things in temperance.

To "temper" is to meld white with black, hot with cold, light with dark. To temper ourselves we need to recognize and accept our light energy as well as our dark energy, our Godselves and our Shadow selves. Through the power of our wills, we can meld our ener-

gies and temper ourselves. Cultivating temperance is
another expression for the ongoing process of seeking
balance within ourselves and takes into consideration
"losing our tempers" so we may reestablish balance
again.

To cultivate temperance you need only to surrender your personal will to that power in you that is Universal Will. Slow the mind, perhaps through meditation, and listen. Listen carefully to what is within and
outside you. Practice listening. In the silence you create you will hear many things in many ways. Sense the
rhythm, the pulse of the stillness. This is your rhythm
and the rhythm of Universal Energy.

Timing is the compliment to temperance. Through
astrology we can discover and identify timing as a reflection of an individual life unfolding. The movement
of the planets in the sky today corresponds to and reflects the expression of energy in the birth chart. Each
planet has its own pattern of motion and rate of speed.
The unfolding of the potential in each birth chart can
be measured by the natural movement of the planets
in concert with each other.

You can also cultivate an ear for your personal timing similar to that described above. Listening to what
is within and around you, sensing the rhythm and
breath of your own energy as an expression of Universal Energy will, with practice, enable you to sense your
right timing.

Through temperance and timing, you align and
attune your life pattern with the flow of Universal Energy. Your natural flow is perfectly synchronized with
the temperance and timing of all of nature.

10. *Live Moment to Moment*

Live moment to moment. Live in the present moment. How often that message is presented, cloaked in mystique and offered almost as a challenge to the real and the possible. Monks, mystics, and New Age philosophers have written a great deal about living moment to moment or living in the present moment. Living moment to moment is regarded by many as the ultimate way of experiencing life.

Living in the present moment, requires focus, attention, and centeredness. Living moment to moment is an ongoing, conscious choice. It is continuous choosing to accept your life as it unfolds. It is surrendering to and being responsible for and to each day, each hour, and each minute of your unique life pattern.

Living moment to moment is an experience, a way of life, available to each one of us. The process is simple but not necessarily easy. Living moment to moment is simple in that it merely requires your conscious choice and establishing a pattern in which to practice continually making the choice. It is choosing and making a habit of choosing.

The "not necessarily easy" part of "simple but not easy" is acceptance and surrender. Acceptance requires your belief. It requires trust that your life pattern as it unfolds is exactly right for you – remember, in spirit, you chose it. Surrender requires turning over your humanness, your ego, to your Godself, the Universal Energy Force of which you are a unique, but complete, expression. It also requires that you understand that you are a part of the constantly changing Universal

Energy in the cycle of life, death, and rebirth.

Some of us chose life patterns where we simply need to understand how this process works in order to put it into practice in life. Others of us chose patterns requiring our actual living out and experiencing, through lessons and life situations, the way to living moment to moment.

My understanding came through the experiencing route. In the last four years of my past life, or Part 1, I was constantly faced with death and dying. As an astrologer I knew that my life pattern was being heavily influenced by the planet Pluto, an influence that would last, for me, a total of about six years. I know that Pluto symbolizes death and rebirth. It represents the concept of power and the universal force of change, especially regarding energy that runs through the cycle of change from life, death, and rebirth.

For four years I fought what I knew I knew. I resisted. I denied. I beat myself up for not being able to change my fate. Why, with all my training, especially in the application of metaphysical principles, could I not turn my life around? Why didn't positive thinking help me get things under control? Why couldn't I get a break? Why was everything and everyone in my life dying? Why was I dying?

I got into a personal power struggle with Pluto and everything the planet reflected in my life. When I began to experience that my life was out of control, I tried to control everything and everyone around me. The more I resisted the power of the Pluto influence, the more I got back control and abuse. I understood that the Pluto energy often brought experiences of facing your own powerlessness, ego powerlessness, the understanding I resisted the most. I let myself be influenced by others who told me that I should snap out of it, be more positive, and rise above my circumstances. I got caught in a self-destructive spiral of resisting my circumstances; desperately trying to get control, most often by doing more and doing it better; and fighting depression and hopelessness.

In four years there was one loss on top of another with little time in between to grieve. My efforts to keep control set up a strong pattern of resistance. By the time I began to stop resisting, it was too late to stop the destructive energy that was being reflected back to me. When it all bottomed out and I said I quit and simply could not go any farther, no one listened. I came face-to-face with the raw nature of the planet Pluto's power to struggle for survival. This coincided with Pluto's movement across a critical point in my birthchart. Astrologers in India, who use a fatalistic approach, would interpret this to be the end of my life sometime in the coming year. The Western interpretation is that of experiencing death and then rebirth.

I had four years of loss and deaths. I now had to face the possibility of my own death in the coming year. Because of my own unique life pattern, the first Pluto influence of four years resulted in my losing or separating from almost everyone and everything I had cared about. The next and immediate influence of Pluto signified my own death and possible rebirth. I had done just about everything and experienced the full range of human experiences in forty-eight years. I had a sense of completion, that things had come full circle with very little unfinished business. I felt okay about dying; yet I instinctively chose life. I chose rebirth but knew I would be caught in an existential trap if I continued my old pattern of resisting, in this case, my own death. The dilemma brought everything into sharp focus. It was the sharp focus of living in the moment.

Living with the heightened awareness of the possibility of your own death narrows your attention down to daily living. I had always understood physical death to be the mere passing from the physical energy plane to the spiritual energy plane. Over the past four years I had actually experienced my understanding.

Out of the absence of fear of death and the acceptance of its possibility for me, life lived day-to-day and moment-to-moment is more precious and special. The simple things are pleasing. Lightness and ease have come to replace the resistance and control of the past. Pluto, with its power to create a long, dark journey of the soul, is also capable of delivering the soul to higher, solid ground.

How to Live In Love

1. Love Yourself and Who You Are. Completely, Totally and Unconditionally.

2. Rediscover your dreams and follow them.

3. Recognize your conditioning and set about to RECONDITION yourself.

4. Seek out and surround yourself with positive people.

5. Express your sense of humor.

6. Use the thought/feeling connection to your best advantage.

7. Keep moving forward.

8. Make a commitment to live SIMPLY, HARMLESSLY, and GRACIOUSLY.

9. Cultivate temperance and timing.

10. Live Moment to Moment.

The Challenge ————————————————

Over the course of the next three years, the planets of Universal fate and destiny, Uranus, Neptune, and Pluto, will, with all the certainty of the change inherent in Universal Energy, present us with the potential of a new age, the Age of Aquarius.

The Piscean Age began during the time of one of Planet Earth's great teachers, Jesus Christ. As a teacher, he taught by example and his three greatest messages — simplicity, compassion, and awareness of spiritual (or cosmic) connectedness framed the meaning of the entire Piscean Age.

The Piscean Age is also the Age of the Patriarchy. The epoch was marked by a shift from the emphasis on female energy in the preceding Age of the Matriarchy, to a predominance of male energy. The Age of Aquarius offers the potential for equilibrium. We sense the press of the planets' forward motion and we are anxious to move on and hurl ourselves into the promise of a new age and a fresh start. But, not so fast.

At the end of the Age of Pisces, while the outer planets of Uranus, Neptune, And Pluto, touch off the

last degree's of their current zodiac signs, we find that
we have unfinished business and endings to attend to.
As we leave this 2100 year epoch, we find ourselves in
a transition phase. Did we learn the Piscean lessons of
simplicity, compassion, and spiritual/cosmic connectedness? Are we prepared for the possibilities offered
by the new Age of Aquarius?

Within the essence of the Pisces energy is contained our greatest hopes and visions and our darkest
shadows and fears. Did we dream our greatest dreams
and build our greatest visions for the future? Did we
expose and conquer our greatest fears?

Pluto's move into Sagittarius at the end of 1995
signals a call for the beginning of a great healing. It is
a time to both heal and be healed. It is the energy of
opportunity for restoring balance of the elements —
fire, earth, air, and water, and balance of the female
and male energies.

Uranus moves into Aquarius in 1996 and begins
to offer support energy for the balancing of male and
female energy and individual creativity. This will be
helpful for our culture and its deep-seated fear of individualism, especially our cultural fear of strong, inde-
pendent women.

Finally, Neptune moves into Aquarius in 1997 al-
lowing plenty of time for individuals to reexamine and
reignite their dreams. This transition is also the time
of the emergence of many spiritual teachers and vi-
sionaries.

During the Pisces Age our culture evolved around
the Pisces impetus for symbiosis and codependency.
Christ was viewed as the great Savior. Our cultural

institutions — governments, religions, schools, and universities have created and perpetuated the perception of being great Saviors. We have a huge conglomerate of vocational professions known collectively as "the helping professions."

The Pisces message of selfless service is noble and was probably best exemplified early in the age through the actual life of Jesus. However, much that was built upon early noble intentions has become corrupt or is reaching a point of diminishing returns. The relationship between our institutions and the people they serve is codependent. Our Savior institutions are far too powerful and dependent on victims to save — the people. In turn, the people, victims, have given over their power to institutions for the promise of rescue. The strong carry the weak. The problem is, neither party can make good on the promise. Our culture has tipped way out of balance and is unhealthy. The transition from the Age of Pisces to the Age of Aquarius is a time of challenge. The Challenge is in two parts.

First, individuals must begin to commit themselves to personal healing. To commit to personal healing is to recognize that your healing affects everyone and everything else in the Universal web. The greatest gift you can give yourself is the gift of balance and wholeness.

Second, people of courage must step forward and act on their individual convictions. I believe it is primarily up to women to make this transformation step happen. Men who have healed and balanced their female and male energies are important in the process; but they cannot make it happen for women. The action must first come from women. Women must claim their respect and value. Many of our groups and organizations, as we know them today, are of no help here. Self-empowered women of courage must stand and must stand alone.

Self-empowerment is complete acceptance of all aspects of yourself. It comes from knowing that you are a perfect expression of Universal Energy, your Godself, in a unique and very human form.

As more and more women have the courage to stand alone, the true Aquarian energy of *standing alone together* will emerge. When both women and men of courage are standing alone together we realize the social structure of the New Age — a society of equal individuals, the Age of Aquarius.

Afterword by Winks

Hi, I'm the little black female miniature schnauzer who has been on this journey for the past year now. I'm the petmate. My proper name is Moonwinks, although I'm Winks to most others, "The Winkster" to a close few, and "Ms. Winks" when I need to be. I'm a sociable ladypup who stands as high as a footstool while projecting the regal bearing of a Great Dane. I'm a capable guardian and I have a fierce streak I can call on when I need it. So far, I haven't had to because I'm pretty good at repelling "bad dogs".

I am Everydog and, moreso, I'm an old soul. I've been around quite a few times and usually alternate lifetimes between being a human being and a dog. I prefer the dog lives and usually see them as a reward for having completed a human life. In fact, I suggest you look at it that way also. I'll tell you why in a little bit.

First, though, I want to tell you about natural leadership. I spent my past human life as a natural leader and decided to spend this new dog-reward life with a human who would help me communicate what I've learned.

The world is in about as much of a crisis as it was over 2,000 years ago when J.C. spent his 33 years here. Yes, I did a stint in dog life back then and, bow-wow, do I see a lot of similarities to the state of things now as to then. My biggest concern some 2,000 years later is that we still don't know how to identify and value leaders. It is even more of an upside-down world today and we keep looking at the wrong stuff. We say, "Don't judge a book by its cover," "Don't judge by outward appearances," but we do it anyway. I know it is easier that way. When I was a human I saw how easy it was to blame others when you operate that way. In the dog world we aren't offered that escape route. My only recourse on encountering "bad dogs" is to bite their legs off.

From my past life as a natural leader, let me give you some short-haired pointers

1. Natural leaders lead by example. Their lives are driven by the quest for excellence in both themselves and others.

2. Natural leaders are all different. That's the point. They are unique individuals. There isn't one place you go to find them. Often the most obvious places, the traditional positions of leadership, are the last places you'll find natural leaders. Once in a while, though, you hit it lucky. Don't count on the political world for much help. Natural leaders seem to be developing allergic reactions to politics these days and I think that is a healthy thing. In my past human life, I briefly invested some of my natural leadership in the political world and had a nasty reaction

that took lots of antibiotics to clear up. Antibiotics were effective back then.

3. Natural leaders are often good communicators. Many are good with words. In a culture that loves words and prides itself on rationality, watch out. We want to believe. Oh, how we want to believe. While some may use words to tell us what we want to hear, don't give your power away for just words. Without corresponding action, words are empty promises.

4. Many natural leaders are quiet and unassuming. Most of the time they lead through compassion and gentleness realizing that even Jesus had to go a little berserk when he encountered that outrageous money-changing deal in the temple.

5. Don't confuse natural leaders with loners or free spirits. Natural leaders are natural lovers and they especially delight in the company of other natural leaders. They understand unconditional love and have the courage to express it as "tough love" when necessary.

6. Natural leaders are ordinary people who often have some extraordinary talents or abilities and often have a special vision. Don't confuse the ordinary person in them with their special talents or vision. They break just like everyone else. They are loyal and usually their biggest hurt comes from betrayal. They aren't stronger than others. They don't have a higher tolerance for pain. They aren't perfect. In fact, a natural leader is usually readily willing to admit mistakes and correct errors.

7. Natural leaders inspire others to be all they can

be. They recognize that each person is unique and encourage the best qualities in everyone.

8.   Natural leaders are often demanding, but only of the simplest of things such as honesty, keeping agreements, and trustworthiness. Natural leaders don't blame and don't accept excuses.

9. Natural leaders don't ask you to give your power over to them. They know that the only person your power works for is you. There are, of course, many in leadership positions who have been good students and pose as natural leaders. Sometimes it is difficult to tell right away.

Natural leaders encourage and support your personal empowerment. In a world used to secret motives and hidden agendas, natural leaders are sometimes misunderstood, highly suspect, or disbelieved because they operate openly. Those posing as leaders manipulate, use others' power for their own purposes, and have hidden agendas and secret motives. Natural leaders inspire personal power in others. Those posing as leaders deplete and disempower others.

10. In the end, natural leaders endure because they are naturals and they inspire though the example of their own lives.

Thanks for the opportunity to share what I learned in my last human lifetime. I hope it is helpful. Now I'll tell you what I have come to see that humans have a little backward. A dog life is generally far superior to a human life. Oh, sure, there are exceptions. I've gotten pretty good at picking circumstances that offer a really good lifestyle and I'm always willing to reciprocate with my human caregiver(s). Believe me, I give lots back and I love to give. I mean, that's what it's all about, isn't it?

My real point is . . . in a dog life all you have to be is a dog. We get to be ourselves from the time we are pups and that is all we are ever expected to be ("bad dogs" excluded). All we have to do is be. And, all we have to be is loyal and unconditionally loving. What could be simpler? I'm amused by humans who say, "It's a dog's life." What could be better? And to those who say, "All dogs do is eat, sleep, and chase their tails (play) all day," my response is "You don't really get it." Aside from the fact that we also spend a great deal of time wondering, a very pleasant state, we exist as examples of what humans can aspire to. We are sort of like heaven on earth.

The next time you are in meditation, contemplating your navel, float this question into the Universe — How does a human become more doglike? You see, most dogs are natural leaders.

I welcome comments and questions from both humans and canines. Felines? I like them. I just don't understand them, but who really does? I'll give it a try, though. Write me at LightHeart Books.

ONCE AROUND THE WHEEL
Want To Go Again?
Life, Death, Healing, Transformation, and Life Again

by Lynne Rich

Additional copies of **ONCE AROUND THE WHEEL, Want to Go Again?** are available for $15.00 ($12.99 plus P&H).

Also available:

Guide for Healing and Transformation — resource for books, tools, and techniques — $11.00

Your Birthchart, a self-help approach to understanding your horoscope — $11.00

_____

Total $

___ # Copies **ONCE AROUND THE WHEEL . . .** _____

___ # Copies **Guide for Healing & Transformation**_____

___ # Copies ***Your Birthchart**   _____

Total Enclosed _____

Name: _____

Address: _____

City: _____ State: _____ Zip: _____

* For each copy of **Your Birthchart**, include:

Name: _____

Date of Birth: _____Time of Birth: _____ a.m. or p.m.

Place of Birth: _____

Send to:

LightHeart Books
P. O. Box 2430-1009
Pensacola, FL 32513-2430